LOOKING FOR LAZARUS

A PREVIEW
OF THE
RESURRECTION

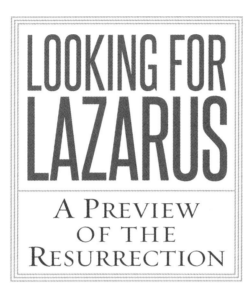

LOOKING FOR LAZARUS

A PREVIEW OF THE RESURRECTION

REGIS MARTIN

Scepter

Published by Scepter Publishers, Inc.
info@scepterpublishers.org
www.scepterpublishers.org
800-322-8773
New York

Cover image: Detail of *Raising Lazarus* by © Eric Wallis, oil on canvas, 33x43 in.
Cover and page design by Rose Design

Library of Congress Control Number: 2021937657
ISBN paperback: 978-1-59417-426-1
ISBN eBook: 978-1-59417-427-8

Printed in the United States of America

For Roseanne Marie Martin

With Love and Gratitude

Old men ought to be explorers

Here and there does not matter

We must be still and still moving

Into another intensity

For a further union, a deeper communion

Through the dark cold and the empty desolation,

The wave cry, the wind cry, the vast waters

Of the petrel and the porpoise. In my end
is my beginning.

Four Quartets

—T. S. Eliot

CONTENTS

PROLOGUE

I f life is a journey, then, at some point surely, it will all come to an end. It cannot go on forever. Certainly not in this world. *Sooner or later all things must die, / And so to dust their bodies fly.*[1] With every rise and fall of the sea—the harsh, implacable sea—we find ourselves drawn nearer and nearer to death. "The bright day is done," Shakespeare reminds us, "And we are for the dark."[2]

Unless, that is, God himself were to reach down from the fastness of Heaven and pull us right out of the water. Will he condescend to do so, rescuing us from a final fall, an everlasting lapse into the nothingness whence we came? If not, then, we are surely bound for the dark, our brief candles snuffed out in the great sea of death. Whether we like it or not, we shall be forced to face the Great Unknown, "the undiscovered country," Shakespeare calls it, "from whose bourne no traveler returns."[3]

---

1. I am not a poet but now and again I may, with a line or two of lyric, impersonate one.

2. *Anthony and Cleopatra*, act 5, scene 2.

3. *Hamlet*, act 3, scene 1.

And when will the dread nightfall begin? The short answer is: at birth, which for every parent of every child has always meant the promised dawn of new life. But it is not so. That roseate picture postcard of every child's future is no more to be trusted than the waxen wings of poor Icarus. How smooth the takeoff, you think, and sweet; only to end in abject defeat. "We have a winding-sheet in our mother's womb," warns the great spell-binder John Donne, whose sermons kept even the king in thrall, "and we come into the world wound up in that winding-sheet, for we come to seek a grave . . . we celebrate our own funerals with cries even at our birth."[4]

And yet, notwithstanding Donne's dread summons, is the claim in fact true? Are there really no exceptions to the universality of death? Must life always be a thing as vaporous as the dew, its fragility no more than fallen leaves driven by the wind? Is humankind but a field of dry grass beneath a broiling sun, fated only to wither and die? Because, this side of mythology, there really was someone who did manage to escape,

---

4. "Death's Duel," Donne's last sermon, preached before the king shortly before Donne's death on March 31, 1631.

to resist the downward pull, and thus found himself strangely returned from the realm of the dead. His name was Lazarus, whose candle had clearly gone out and yet, for all that, God brought him back from the undiscovered country.

There is an entire chapter of Sacred Scripture given over to the story of Lazarus, an eyewitness account, no less, told by the beloved disciple of Jesus himself, St. John the Divine, whom pious tradition calls "the clear-eyed eagle," because he saw more deeply into the things of God than any living man. The dramatic details of his rising and return from the grave are the centerpiece of chapter eleven of John's Gospel, a tale told in forty-six thrilling verses.

It is within those few stirring lines of narration that we find all that we require to remind us of a force stronger than death, an aura brighter than the sun and the stars.

Love.

Which moves not merely sun and moon and stars, but the whole blooming universe as well. From the angels up above to the amoebas down below, an entire circuitry of life created and sustained by an absolute and eternal love. "Love is itself unmoving," T. S. Eliot tells us, sounding the Johannine theme by way of Dante: "Only the cause and end of movement."[5] Why should not God, therefore, who is love through and through, be able to exercise a power sufficient to vanquish the dust of the earth and the darkness of sin?

"Love bade me welcome: yet my soul drew back, / Guilty of dust and sin." So begins "Love," by the poet George Herbert, consisting of fourteen lines of stunning verse, in which neither dust nor sin can thwart Christ's astonishing invitation: "You must sit down, says Love, and taste my meat." And so, moved by the grace of God's own hospitality, the soul allows itself to be persuaded to set aside its heavy load of scrupulosity, and simply says yes: "So I did sit and eat."[6] How well Albert Camus put it when he wrote: "It is not with scruples that a man grows tall. Like a beautiful day, height is given according to God's will."[7]

Thus, when the Apostle Paul announces in his Letter to the Corinthians, "Death is swallowed up in

5. T. S. Eliot, "Burnt Norton." *Four Quartets* (New York: Harcourt, Brace, 1943), section V, lines 166–167.

6. George Herbert, "Love (III)," in *Herbert: Poems*, ed. Peter Washington (New York: Alfred A. Knopf, 2004).

7. Albert Camus, *Notebooks* 1951–1959, trans. Ryan Bloom (Chicago: Ivan R. Dee, 2008), p. 26.

victory. . . . O death, where is thy sting?" (1 Cor 15:54–55), it is not any sort of figure of speech he is spinning. Nor is he indulging in wishful thinking, like the frightened boy who whistles bravely while hurrying past a cemetery. It is instead absolute certitude and consolation that he offers, the possession of which is what finally matters. Until we decide to cling to that rock, no amount of happiness or wealth in this world can compensate us for the loss of eternal life in the next. That is the whole point of the Johannine story, and one we must never tire of telling.

The story of Lazarus is one of those drop-everything tales, which needs to be told exactly as the apostle John has given it to us, along with as much wisdom we have the wit to tease out of it. So, what does it mean to me, an old man who finds himself poised ever more precariously along that razor's edge, beyond which the looming and fearful presence of death beckons? One mustn't keep the Angel of Death waiting too long. And why shouldn't I want to wrestle with him? After all, if I refuse, unlike the prophet Jacob who, following a long night spent in wrestling with *his* angel, would not desist until he'd extracted a blessing, there will be no blessing for me. So, let there be a duel, if not to the death, at least to some closure concerning what I take to be its meaning. Let me at least try and shake the tree a little bit, hoping a modest blessing or two may fall, revealing something of the Old Guy—Death—first of the Four Last Things ever to be remembered.

As for the others—Judgment, Heaven, Hell—they will follow only after we have faced the first, death, the threatened cancellation of all that we have and hope to carry with us into eternity. It is the common fate of all us mortals. *The Big Sleep*, Raymond Chandler has called it, from which he certainly had no expectation of ever awakening.[8] And I, who devoutly believe he was mistaken (and knows better now), why should I not wish to try and disabuse others of the same mistake? Especially with the Old Guy peering ever more closely over my shoulder? He may not have contacted me directly by phone, like those doddering old fools found in Muriel Spark's *Memento Mori*, who react with senile resentment each time he calls, however salutary the summons: "*Remember you must die.*"[9]

---

8. Raymond Chandler, *The Big Sleep* (New York: Alfred A. Knopf, 1939).

9. A delightful whodunit, starring Death as the chief character. Published in 1959 by Lippincott, making both her and her story famous.

Why not, then, try and set down a few items of faith by which to navigate our final passage "We go to the Father of souls," St. Cyril of Jerusalem reminded his catechumens, "but in order to do so it is necessary to pass by the Dragon."[10] It is the journey we've all embarked upon, and its outcome, in the perspective of hope, is to see the face of God and thus to be embraced forever by the arms of his Son, Jesus, who has shown us how to live and to die. What else is there to hope for if not the happy discovery of finding God on the other side of death? The very one, faith tells us, who is waiting to see us.

There is a moving prayer by François Mauriac, one of the great writers of Catholic France, which I often say:

> Grant, O Lord, that I may lose myself in the peace of thy presence, so that when my hour comes, I shall pass through a transition almost insensible, from you to you, from you the living bread, the

---

10. Cyril of Jerusalem, *The Works of Saint Cyril of Jerusalem*, vol. 1 (Washington, DC: Catholic University of America Press, 1969), 82. Quotation is a paraphrase of St. Cyril's original: "In your journey to the Father of Souls, your way lies past that dragon. How shall you pass him? You must have 'your feet stoutly with the gospel of peace' so that, even if he does bite you, he may not hurt you." Paraphrased epigraph is found here: Flannery O'Connor, *A Good Man is Hard to Find And Other Stories* (New York: Harcourt, Inc., 1948), p. 1.

bread of mankind, to you, the love alive, already possessed by those of my own beloved who have gone before me into thy shelter.[11]

So, then, let's have a look at Lazarus. But why go to John to take that look? Isn't there enough already about old Lazarus in Matthew, Mark, and Luke, the so-called synoptics? Actually, there is nothing, not even a scintilla to suggest that he ever existed. The only point of entry is John, through whose prism we alone are enabled to see anything at all. If there be something like a *figure in the carpet*, to use an expressive image drawn by that master storyteller, Henry James, with which to thread one's way through, then best leave it to the apostle John to thread the needle. And the thing, of course, which especially commends the Johannine account, is the fact that it bears witness, that it provides a singular eyewitness to the truth of the reality of God, of whose enfleshment he, John, and the Gospel he wrote, provide the most profound and intimate testimony. Who besides John, the beloved disciple, can claim such closeness to Christ as to have rested upon his heart at the Last Supper, the night before he died?

11. Found on a Prayer Card for the Deceased. Source unknown.

Another way of putting it is to say that John's Gospel is the most purely spiritual account of Christ that we have, which is how Clement of Alexandria put it back in the late second century. As a result of which, he is often called "the theologian," because he is determined on unearthing the deepest possible meaning beneath the literal level. When you peel away the surface details, what survives? What remains most real and fundamental, *the* most deeply abiding sense regarding all that Christ said or did? When Jesus, for instance, tells Nicodemus that he must be "born again," what does that mean? Or in the encounter with the woman at the well, whose attention is suddenly drawn, her thirst elevated, to the possibility of "living water," what does Jesus mean in speaking that way? There are depths here which St. John the Divine is supremely qualified to plumb.

In fact, the whole atmospheric world of the Fourth Gospel is strikingly different from anything in the New Testament. Right out of the gate, as it were, John has left the others behind, leaping straight off the page into the sheer otherness of God, where the air is pure and thin with the ether of eternity. St. Augustine, for example, in describing the movements of John's Gospel, tells us that he "soars very high, mounting beyond the darkness of the earth and fixing his gaze on the light of truth."[12] Like a Gothic spire aimed at the heart of God, John is wholly bent on seeing into the things of God, to lay bare the heart of the Savior. Such is the motive power driving the Last Gospel.

Confronted by such sheer verticality, we might almost be forgiven for suspecting John of harboring secret gnostic sympathies, of longing to escape altogether, taking permanent leave of the planet. That is, of course, impossible, because in going up he meets Another, who is coming down, the whole trajectory of whose descent placing him square in the middle of this fallen world, amid the muck and the mire of flesh-bound human beings. John's Gospel may well strike this sublimely spiritual note at the start, with its insistence that, "In the beginning was the Word, and the Word was with God, and the Word was God," but

---

12. From a stirring tribute paid to the author of what St. Clement of Alexandria called "the spiritual gospel." It was he, John the Beloved Apostle, adds Augustine, who "soared beyond the flesh, soared beyond the earth which he trod, beyond the seas which he saw, beyond the air where birds fly; soared beyond the sun, beyond the moon and the stars, beyond all spirits which are unseen, beyond his own intelligence and the very reason of his thinking soul." Cited in *Tractates on the Gospel of John 1–10* (*The Fathers of the Church*, Vol. 78). Translated by John W. Rettig. Catholic University of America Press, 1988.

only in order to tell us—scandalously, unmistakably—
that this very Word "became flesh and made his dwell-
ing among us, and we saw his glory, the glory as of
the Father's only Son, full of grace and truth," who has
come to us from out of the bosom of the Father, from
out of the silence of the heavens, that immense sounding silence of which the saints and mystics speak.[13]

It is, faith tells us, from the fallout of God's glory
that we have all received, grace upon grace. And while
no one has ever seen the Father—excepting, of course,
the Son, who is the fullness and overflow of his Revelation, the living icon of the Father's love—his Word
has come among us precisely in order to speak the
Father's name. And not only to speak his Name, but to
show us the Father whose Name he speaks. Yes, from
all eternity. Isn't this why Jesus reminds Philip, who
first put the question to him, "He who has seen me
has seen the Father"? (Jn 14:9). Because—so Jesus will

---

13. To paraphrase a passage taken from one of seven letters dictated by St.
Ignatius, Bishop and Martyr, on his way to Rome where wild beasts awaited
him in the Colosseum. Intended for the Church in Ephesus, it is his longest
and arguably among the most moving pieces of early Christian literature.
Appointed the second bishop of Antioch, tradition places his death some-
time during the reign of Trajan (98 to 117 AD), the emperor who ordered his
execution. Quotations from Jn 1:1, 14.

insist—"I and the Father are one" (Jn 10:30). Christ, you see, has made him present, palpably present, merciful and powerful before men—one of whom (Lazarus by name) languishes amid the darkness of death. It is he Christ will go to and set free. . . .

CHAPTER I

On the Lookout for Lazarus

Now a certain man was ill, Lazarus of Bethany, the village of Mary and her sister Martha. It was Mary who anointed the Lord with ointment and wiped his feet with her hair, whose brother Lazarus was ill. So the sisters sent to him, saying, "Lord, he whom you love is ill."

—Jn 11:1–3

Here are the facts as we know them, cobbled together by a master wordsmith, St. John the Divine, who places them right at the beginning of chapter eleven. A perfectly plain account, by the way, no attempt having been made to embroider upon the event. A man named Lazarus falls ill and his two sisters, Martha and Mary, send word to Jesus to come and heal him. We are not told how ill, only that it was serious enough to warrant an appeal to Jesus whom, we are told, loves Lazarus. And yet, oddly enough, he does not come, at least not at once. And when Jesus does finally set out, two days later, the poor man is dead.

Did Jesus not know this? After all, he is God. Meanwhile, how strangely the rest of us are affected by the news of his death. It quite endears him to us, owing no doubt to the fact that in the end we shall all be dead. Unless, of course, the mortality rate has suddenly dropped below 100 percent. Quoting the late Philip Roth, who lifted the line from Kafka, "The meaning of life is that it stops." It was a line which he'd often repeat—until, that is, his own life stopped.[1] "Birth, and copulation, and death," writes T. S. Eliot, "That's all the facts when you come to brass tacks." Thanks for letting us know, Mr. Eliot. Yes, we shall all be alone at the end, "waiting for a knock and the turning of a lock for you know the hangman's waiting for you."[2]

---

1. Daniel Sandstrom, "My Life As A Writer" (Interview with Philip Roth), *The New York Times*, March 2, 2014, *http://www.nytimes.com/2014/03/16/books/review/my-life-as-a-writer.html*.

2. Eliot, "Sweeney Agonistes," *Collected Poems* 1909–1962 (New York: Harcourt, Brace & Co., 1963), p. 131.

All because man is a being born to die. Because, more to the point, man alone knows he must die. The animals do not know this. They are not, like us, blest with self-consciousness. Not even in the midst of their dying can they detach themselves sufficiently from the event to reflect on its meaning. It is for us alone to entertain thoughts and fears of impending extinction—indeed, to see death as really the most commonplace of all happenings. What could be more banal, more drearily obvious than the fact that everyone will die? As someone once said, it is only down streets marked by graves that any of us make our way into the world of the past. At the same time, however, is death not the most painfully incomprehensible, the least welcome of all that conspires to overtake and destroy us? "On pain of death, let no man name death to me: it is a word infinitely terrible," to quote a character from John Webster's *The White Devil*, destined himself for a most horrible death.[3]

Asked once by an interviewer what bothered him most about life, the poet Robert Lowell answered very simply: "That people die."[4] But how newsworthy a

---

3. John Webster, *The White Devil*, ed. John Russell Brown (Manchester and New York: Manchester University Press, 1977), 5.3.39–40.

4. Regis Martin, *The Last Things: Death, Judgment, Hell, Heaven* (San Francisco: Ignatius Press, 1998).

datum is that? Can there honestly be anyone on the planet who does not yet know people die, that all things living must die? "We are all born," observes Joseph Epstein, "with a serious and unalterable birth defect: we grow old—at least the lucky among us do—and then we die."[5] Is there a single sentient being out there prepared to take exception to that universal truth?

"It is the blight man was born for," says the narrator of "Spring and Fall," a haunting poem by Gerard Manley Hopkins, SJ, in which a young girl innocently wanders into a forest full of dying leaves. And when, unaccountably, she begins to weep, the narrator wants to know why. "Margaret," he asks,

> are you grieving
> Over Goldengrove unleaving?
> Leaves, like the things of man, you
> With your fresh thoughts care for. . . .

And with brutal finality, he tells her: "It is the blight man was born for, / It is Margaret you mourn for."[6]

---

5. *A Literary Education and Other Essays* (Edinburg, Va.: Axios, 2014), p. 143.

6. Gerard Manley Hopkins, "Spring and Fall," *Poems of Gerard Manley Hopkins*, ed. Robert Bridges (London: Humphrey Milford, 1918).

If death is the fate that awaits us in the end, sickness will be the road on which we are most likely to travel. "All my life," Flannery O'Connor was wont to say, "death and suffering have been brothers to my imagination."[7] (As Thomas Merton said of her when she died: "Her pen had been dipped in pain.") Indeed, she had never been anywhere but sick, a place, she called it, "more instructive than a long trip to Europe . . . a place . . . where nobody can follow."[8]

Isn't that what especially strikes us about Lazarus? Not just that he's ill, but that in the condition of his being ill, he's one of us, he is *Everyman*. Thus, with repeated hammer blows, John's Gospel hits us head-on with the news of our shared brokenness. That in the end we must all stare unblinkingly before the face of death, forced to endure the loss and the silence it brings. Epstein mordantly reminds us that death "is an old joke that comes to each of us afresh . . . and that old age is the straight man who prepares us, always inadequately, for the punch line."[9]

---

7. Regis Martin, "Flannery O'Connor—Fifty Years After," *Crisis Magazine*, July 31, 2014, *www.crisismagazine.com/2014/flannery-oconnor-fifty-years*.

8. Flannery O'Connor, *The Habit of Being* (New York: Farrar, Straus and Giroux, 1988), letter of June 28, 1956.

9. Epstein, p. 148.

So who is this poor fellow Lazarus, for whom two sisters will mobilize all their resources to summon the Lord? He plainly cannot speak for himself; rather like St. Joseph, spouse of the Blessed Virgin, his life is defined by silence. And yet he is greatly loved by Jesus, which surely distinguishes him among his neighbors and friends, who may not even have heard of Jesus. That and, of course, the blessing of two remarkable sisters, the practical Martha and the prayerful Mary, whose company Jesus often came to Bethany to share. Now especially, when word having gone out to Jesus, he must surely rush back to comfort and heal his friend. How can he refuse so blithe, so beguiling an appeal? Here are the two sides of the Church, active and contemplative, combining their gifts to urge Jesus to bring solace and healing to his friend, to his friend's family. Indeed, to all who, like Lazarus, are sick and in need of help.

Why doesn't he come? I mean, at once and without hesitation? Here is one of those mysteries that will not yield to cheap or immediate solution. Death is not like a problem in arithmetic, and we must not impose a solution as though it were just a matter of crunching numbers. Nor may we imagine for a moment that because Jesus has not roused himself at once on behalf of a broken world, that he is either asleep or indifferent. It is not a mere facile faith that teaches us that God always hears the cry of those who suffer, or that no prayer goes unanswered. It is also salutary to remind ourselves that even his own prayer when, in the awful anguish of the Garden while his disciples slept, he cried aloud to God, seemed not to have been answered, either.

➤ Loving Father, solace of all who suffer, come
   quickly, we pray, to comfort and restore
   a broken and fallen world, which only you
   can make whole.

CHAPTER 2

The Languishing
of Lazarus

But when Jesus heard it he said, "This illness is not unto death; it is for the glory of God, so that the Son of God may be glorified by means of it." Now Jesus loved Martha and her sister and Lazarus. So when he heard that he was ill, he stayed two days longer in the place where he was.

—Jn 11:4–6

When a friend or wife cries out for help, what do we do? Wait until the commercial comes along, so that the TV show will not be unduly interrupted? Tell them to look elsewhere for help? Of course not. We are expected to drop everything and rush to the stricken side of those we love. Or, in the case of a stranger, we rush to someone we do not love—at least not until we've gotten to know him, which could well happen after we show up. Like the Good Samaritan in Luke's Gospel, who, on seeing the stranger by the side of the road, goes at once to try and relieve his sufferings, refusing to leave until he'd spent an entire night ministering to him, then settling all future accounts with the innkeeper the next day. Hardly an ordinary exercise in conventional medical care, is it? Even dedicated doctors these days do not do house calls, never mind the urgency of the need. Let 9-1-1 look into it.

So, what's keeping Jesus? Why doesn't he drop everything and come straightaway? We are certainly left in no doubt about the relationship here. Jesus truly loves Lazarus, whose need for him could not have been more exigent. Who knows, perhaps in his last moments, Lazarus cried out to his friend, invoking the familiar Aramaic phrase, *Maranatha*, which simply means: "O Lord, come!" Yet, it seems not to have done him any good at all. Where is the evidence of any comparable concern on Christ's part? The Lord, it would appear, has given the matter no priority whatsoever. Why otherwise would he delay in coming, dawdling "for two days," we are told, "in the place where he was"? What was so pressing that he could not leave off doing it for the sake of someone he loved? Someone for whom no joy would have been greater than the heart-felt hope that Christ would come?

But he does not come. Clearly, then, from the evidence of the text, his behavior is, at the very least, inexplicable. Worse, it appears to have been intolerable. We want to shake our fist at God. Grab him by the lapels, as it were, and say to him, "Why won't you come? What are you waiting for?" We think of poor Teresa of Avila, who, notwithstanding repeated pleas to God while struggling across a flooded river, very nearly drowns before reaching the other side. "If this is how you treat your friends," she yells at God, "it is no wonder you have so few!"[1]

There are worse stories, to be sure. Far worse. For instance, the deadly tempest that caused the wreck of the *Deutschland*, its last hours immortalized in thirty-five stanzas of heart-stopping verse by Gerard Manley Hopkins.[2] There, at the epicenter of its

---

1. See the *Life of St. Teresa*, a 1912 translation by Alice Lady Lovat of a French Carmelite nun's account, which validates the story on page 548. The event took place in January of 1582, the last year of Teresa's life.

2. Gerard Manley Hopkins, "Wreck of the Deutschland," in *Poems of Gerard Manley Hopkins*, ed. Robert Bridges (London: Humphrey Milford, 1918).

impacted violence, stands a tall, gaunt Franciscan nun, her voice rising above the storm's tumult, above even the terrified cries of the passengers and crew, crying out repeatedly, "O Christ, Christ, come quickly!"

But did he come? No, he did not. Not certainly between the dark hours of midnight and dawn when the ship, wave upon wave having "rolled on her beam with ruinous shock,"[3] at last breaks apart on a sandbank at the entrance to the Thames Estuary, pitching hundreds of hapless human beings into the sea, including five Franciscan nuns exiled from their native land. "Rhine refused them," lamented Hopkins, referencing the religious persecution which drove them to flee Bismarck's Germany, only to fall prey to the caprices of an English sea: "Thames would ruin them."[4]

"Away in the loveable west," writes Hopkins, safely ensconced in Wales where, "under a roof here, I was at rest":

And they the prey of the gales;
She to the black-about air, to the breaker, the
    thickly
Falling flakes to the throng that catches and quails,

---

3. Hopkins, "Wreck of the Deutschland," stanza 14, line 110.
4. Hopkins, "Wreck of the Deutschland," stanza 21, line 163.

Was calling "O Christ, Christ, come quickly":
The cross to her she calls Christ to her, christens
    her wild-worst Best.[5]

We are reminded, once again, of those last anguished hours spent by poor Lazarus, who awaited Jesus no less lovingly than did those doomed souls lost at sea. So, to repeat the refrain, why didn't he come sooner? What possible impediment could there have been to prevent his leaving at once on hearing the news? Why would Jesus wish his friend to languish alone so near to death? Such delay seems both strange and, yes, quite heartless. A kind of death sentence, actually. In his great work, *The Lord*, Romano Guardini, one of a handful of truly titanic figures in Catholic theology and today a Servant of God, tells us that in putting off his visit to Lazarus until it is too late to save him, "Jesus does something that seems monstrous: he simply lets Lazarus die."[6] How could he abandon one whom he so dearly loved?

But, then, hadn't he announced in advance that his illness would not end in death, but rather redound to God's own glory? And that here we have a most

---

5. Hopkins, "Wreck of the Deutschland," stanza 24.

6. Quoted in part three: The Decision, chapter 7, "Those Whom He Loved" (Mumbai, India: St. Paul's Press, 1962), p. 192.

mysterious foreshadowing of another death, that of Jesus' own death, toward which he himself is moving, indeed, from the first moment of his conception in the womb of his mother until that last fateful descent into the shame and the silence of the tomb. It is a kind of dress rehearsal for the Mystery of Holy Saturday and, to be sure, the whole trajectory of Christ's life—from womb to tomb—has been a movement toward that very rendezvous he so longed to have, not only with death, but with the awful loneliness that follows. Pope Benedict XVI, in a moving reflection while kneeling before the Shroud of Turin, reminds us of that mystery:

> The Shroud speaks to us precisely about this moment, testifying exactly to that unique and unrepeatable interval in the history of humanity and the universe in which God, in Jesus Christ, not only shared our dying but also our remaining in death— the most radical solidarity.[7]

What other reason could there be, then, for Lazarus to spend two whole days in the tomb, unless it were

---

7. Benedict XVI, Pastoral Visit to Turin: Veneration of the Holy Shroud, Meditation of His Holiness Benedict XVI (May 2, 2010), Vatican website: *www.vatican.va*.

intended to prefigure in some mysterious way the time Christ himself must spend in the nether world? That very sickness unto death which has overtaken Lazarus, will thus serve, in the perspective of hope, as a signpost pointing us to an ultimate restoration. The time spent by Jesus before setting out for Bethany, during which death appears to have undone his friend, will become emblematic of the time of Christ's own entombment, now utterly eclipsed in Easter joy. This is because the Lord Jesus Christ, as we need repeatedly to remind ourselves, most especially amid the darkness and travail of life, remains so entirely and everlastingly real, so intensely alive, that he can actually afford to be dead. He knows how to outrun his own death, and thus in climbing out of the grave he is able to help us survive our own.

Like Lazarus, we too need to rejoice in the saving— albeit hidden and often unfelt—presence of Christ, who comes to rescue us amid the sickness and death that mark our lives.

➤ Come, Father of unending life!
  May we receive in joy your saving presence
  in our lives, lest sickness and death
  leave us forsaken and alone.

CHAPTER 3

Light of the World

Then after this [Jesus] said to the disciples, "Let us go into Judea again." The disciples said to him, "Rabbi, the Jews were but now seeking to stone you, and are you going there again?" Jesus answered, "Are there not twelve hours in the day? If any one walks in the day, he does not stumble, because he sees the light of this world. But if any one walks in the night, he stumbles, because the light is not in him."

—Jn 11:7–10

If my life is a question that can only finally be answered in Christ, then it behooves me to know how Christ lived his life. What choices did he make in the course of living it? How were they determinative of *his* destiny? In other words, what was the answer to the question that defined *his* life? Did he not also need to look to *someone* for the meaning of his own life? Who really was Christ? These are not idle questions. The New Testament tells us unmistakably that he was the Son of the Most High God, wedded from all eternity as the Father's Word, or *Logos*, thus the very ground upon which everything else exists. If there be being, Christ is its meaning. How could he, in the circumstance, be under any sort of compulsion to explain or justify his decisions?

Perhaps not to us, but certainly to the Father. Unless, of course, Christ were sunk in complete solipsism, an absolute monad as it were, subsisting entirely in himself. If he were only that, it would not matter in the least what we, or the world, thought about him. That's because neither we, nor the world, would have existed. Which may account for the following quip, to wit, that if God were only Mind, then never mind. Likewise, if he were only Matter, then nothing matters. Happily, however, God is neither one nor the other. What he is, of course, is a Communion of Persons—distinguished only, as Boethius first reminded us back in the sixth century, by the relations that unite them. "Trinity is secured through the category of relation, and the Unity is maintained through the fact that there is no difference of substance, or operation, or generally of any substantial predicate."[1] The Father is not the Son, nor is the Son the Father, and neither one is the Holy Spirit. Nevertheless, they do breathe forth—"spirate," is how the tradition terms it—the Third Person. "It is not well for God," warns Chesterton, that great quipster, "to be alone."[2]

The bottom line, therefore, is that Christ stands totally in relation to the Father, who, from all eternity, speaks his Word, the sheer Self-Utterance of God. Whether we are grappling with Christ's own identity, or the mission given him to enter and redeem a fallen world, we are to see things always in relation to the Father. Here, says von Balthasar, in a breathtaking formulation, is nothing less than "the historical self-emptying of the eternal self-interpretation of the Father in the Son."[3] The entire orientation of Christ, then, the whole rhythm and thrust of his existence, is to be from the Father, to the Father, and with the

---

1. Anicius Manlius Severinus Boethius, "The Trinity is One God, Not Three Gods," in *Boethius: The Theological Tractates*, trans. H. F. Stewart and E. K. Rand (New York: G. P. Putnam's Sons, 1918).

2. *Orthodoxy* (New York: Dodd, Mead and Company, 1908), p. 252.

3. Veronica Donnelly, *Saving Beauty: Form as the Key to Balthasar's Christology* (New York: Peter Lang, 2007), p. 252.

Father. Who not for a single instant may Christ forget or dismiss. The Father is not to be treated as a parenthetical aside. Rather he is always the point, *the still point*, from whom the Son lives; the point toward whom, *in the turning world*, he turns at every turn. Everything impinging upon his life, and death, necessarily proceeds from above, from the Father.

All right, then. If Christ is this perfect and eternal Word spoken by the Father, then it follows that he has no other Word to speak. It is all contained in one, single, inexhaustible Word. And because God is God, who dwells in light unapproachable, there is no end to the mystery of trying to parse his ways. This is why there can be no biography of Christ, no psychological profile produced on the Incarnate Word. "All one can do," writes Guardini on the first page of his masterful study, *The Lord*, "is demonstrate from ever new points of departure how all attributes, all characteristics of Christ terminate in the incomprehensible, an incomprehensibility, however, of measureless promise."[4]

The exercise of God's freedom, then, is not amenable to analysis, not an area to which we even have

---

4. From the Preface, p. v.

access. Indeed, in the sudden, unforeseen event of his enfleshment, so stunningly shown in the human face of Christ, God manages to conceal even more than he reveals. Here is the Law of Disguise, a principle operative in every circumstance in the life of Christ—and most especially in the Eucharist, whose shape and appearance utterly belie the fact that it is God himself hidden beneath the accidents of bread, water, and wine. And so, as always, decisions made in freedom by Christ, which spring forth from the fullness of his life with the Father, are simply lost amid the precincts of a divine and eternal felicity. They cannot be encompassed by the mind of man. Not even an angelic being can lay bare the mind of God.

"If all things were within our grasp," St. Gregory of Nyssa tells us, whose words apply even to seraphic creatures, "the Higher Power would not be beyond us."[5] Yes, God is intelligible—he does not, as Einstein assures us, "play dice with the universe"—but he is not the least bit comprehensible. "Infinite intelligilibility—such is God," Henri de Lubac insists. Which, he then

---

5. Hans Urs von Balthasar, *Presence and Thought: An Essay on the Religious Philosophy of Gregory of Nyssa* (San Francisco: Ignatius Press, 1995), p. 1.

adds, is precisely why, "The deeper we enter into the infinite, the better we understand that we can never hold it in our hands."[6]

So, when Christ, having blithely announced that he would not be going back to Bethany to see his friend Lazarus, announces that he would instead be returning to Judea, not only are the disciples baffled. The reader is as well. Why? Because the news is simply incomprehensible. Wasn't he nearly killed there? Surely it would be madness to return. Ah, but the counsels of mere human prudence are not for him; his purposes effortlessly transcend the calculations of finite men. Besides, does he not walk while the day is still light? ("Are there not," he asks, "twelve hours in a day?") How then can he stumble? He is, after all, the light of the world: an intensity, no less, of light and life, whose source and duration are equally eternal. Without Christ, therefore, there could be no light, even as he remains the Word without whom no other word may be spoken. There is nothing that can put out this light. And, to be sure, those who walk with him in the light, however strewn with suffering and death their path may be, will neither

---

6. Henri de Lubac, *The Discovery of God*, trans. Alexander Dru (Grand Rapids, Mich.: Wm. B. Eerdmans Publishing Co., 1996), p. 117.

stumble nor fall. For bathed in this light, the radiance of God shall stream forth continuously, quickening the courage of those who choose to follow him, back to the place where "his hour," the Father's hour and his ultimate triumph, awaits him.

Along the way, of course, Christ will see to it that his friend Lazarus shall awaken from the sleep of death.

➤ Heavenly Father, give us the light of your Son, that we too may have the clarity to see and the courage to follow, amid the dark night of faith, the path he first blazed through the world.

CHAPTER 4

Life Vanquishes Death

[Jesus] said to [his disciples], "Our friend Lazarus has fallen asleep, but I go to awake him out of sleep." The disciples said to him, "Lord, if he has fallen asleep, he will recover." Now Jesus had spoken of his death, but they thought that he meant taking rest in sleep.

—Jn 11:11–13

It is entirely understandable that the disciples, on hearing the news that their friend Lazarus has fallen asleep and that Jesus intends to go and wake him, should be left in a state of blithering confusion. After all, if someone is actually asleep, why should it be necessary to have to go and wake him? Is there an appointment somewhere that requires Jesus to go and fetch Lazarus? Of course not. In point of fact, Lazarus is not sleeping at all. He's dead. Which means he's fallen into a state much deeper and certainly more darkly sinister than ordinary sleep.

How *are* the dead, then, to be awakened? That seems like a fair question to put to people whose lives, after all, carry an expiration date. Death does not suddenly become an optional extra just because people decide that they'd rather go on living forever. The moment you start to live, you have begun to die. But, of course, these days not everyone accepts that particular hypothesis, including the author of an exceedingly silly book called *Lifespan: Why We Age and Why We Don't Have To*.[1] Which pretty much tells you all you need to know, namely, the fact that what used to be called the hard truth about the human condition, which is that we shall all die, apparently no longer applies. Has no one told the author that, alas, no one gets out alive? Meanwhile, the book assures us that, "Aging is a disease, and that disease is treatable . . . and that in the near future we may not just be able to *feel* younger but actually *become* younger."

---

1. David Sinclair, *Lifespan: Why We Age and Why We Don't Have To* (New York: Atria, 2019). The later quote is from p. 3.

Cicero certainly got it right in telling us that no man is ever so old as to think that he cannot live another year. For the most part, we willingly acquiesce in theory that the candle will someday go out, that life is not a disease subject to treatment. But as a practical matter we manage to get up each morning convinced that we'll still be around the next day. Or, as Pascal shrewdly reminds us, "We run heedlessly into the abyss after putting something in front of us to stop us seeing it."[2] Which is why, surely, the effort endlessly to extend human life should strike one as, well, insane. Or, at the very least, an exercise in idiocy. Like the fabled geometer in Dante Alighieri's work who tried to square the circle, not realizing that it cannot be done.[3] The Old Guy will not be put off indefinitely. He will have the last word. Isn't that the grim realization to which the knight, in famed director Ingmar Bergman's plague film *The Seventh Seal*, is fatally drawn? Life is not a chess game we can possibly win. However skillfully we succeed in postponing the moment of ultimate checkmate, Death will have us all in the end.

---

2. From the *Pensées* (London: Penguin Limited, 2003), no. 166.

3. Dante Alighieri, *Paradiso*, in *The Comedy of Dante Alighieri, the Florentine*, vol. 3, trans. Dorothy L. Sayers (New York: Penguin, 1949), Canto 33.

Perhaps this is why, after a certain age, sensible folk should refuse, on seeing death, to be surprised. It is, after all, the most commonplace, indeed, the most predictable of events. "Few things," Epstein reminds us, "are less distinguished than death, that most democratic of events."[4] To think that it is I who decide when to die, therefore, is sheer self-conceit and deception. "In the midst of life," says the burial rite from the *Book of Common Prayer*, "we are in death."

There is no talisman, as it were, or magic formula to recite on entering death's door. It will open, to be sure, but it is not a revolving door. To suppose otherwise is the stuff of fantasy, like the fairytales we tell little children to allay their fear of the dark—that darkness which we all know is real and even now surrounds the walls we've thrown up to try and keep it at bay. When people grow up it is understood that they must put away the illusory hopes of little children, who imagine that their parents run the universe for their benefit. And thus must face the fear we all harbor that, at the end of the day, death is but the foreground to an everlasting dark that awaits us all. "The

4. *The Ideal of Culture: Essays* (Edinburg, Va.: Axios, 2018), p. 34.

total emptiness for ever," Philip Larkin calls it in his poem "Aubade."

> The sure extinction that we travel to
> And shall be lost in always. Not to be here,
> Not to be anywhere,
> And soon; nothing more terrible, nothing
>   more true.[5]

It puts one in mind of the story of the little girl named Janet, who, the poet John Crowe Ransom tells us, slept beautifully one day, "Till it was deeply morning."[6] Then, rising at once, she goes in search of her beloved brown hen named Chucky, only to discover that "poor old Chucky" had died in the night, victim of "a transmogrifying bee."

The poor girl is stricken, positively shattered by grief. And turning to her parents, whom she childishly imagines have the power to waken the dead, begs them to bring poor Chucky back to life. "And [she] would

---

5. Philip Larkin, "Aubade," *Collected Poems* (New York: Farrar Straus and Giroux, 2001).

6. John Crowe Ransom, "Janet Waking," *Selected Poems*, 3rd ed. (New York: Alfred A. Knopf, Inc., 1978).

not be instructed," Ransom tells us, "in how deep /
Was the forgetful kingdom of death."

Life, then, is a journey, which goes in only one
direction. It will sooner or later come to an end. No
exemptions, no loopholes for the lucky few. Because
no one is ever lucky enough to get out alive. "Golden
lads and girls all must," says Shakespeare, "As chim-
ney-sweepers, come to dust."[7] The bright day will soon
be done, then will death's reign have begun.

Unless, there were someone possessed of such infinite
power and love as to be able to reach right in and rescue us from the dread finality of death. One whose
perfect capacity to lay hold of death, and thus turn it
all back to life, is foundational to his being God. He
knows that death can have no claim upon him; neither
dust nor death can put him in harm's way, because he
is *the Way*, without whom there can be no way. So that,
in telling his disciples, "Our friend Lazarus is asleep,
but I am going to awaken him," Jesus is putting them
on notice that not only does he stand superior to the
forces of darkness and death, but that he is free to
return to life those whom it pleases him to raise. And,

7. From *Cymbeline*, act 4, scene 2.

to be sure, standing in the shadow of poor Lazarus, a whole universe has fallen asleep, separated from a light that it simply hasn't the power to turn on. We are all waiting, you see, for *Someone* both mighty and merciful enough to bring us light and life.

And yet, notwithstanding the universality of desire, of this deep tenacity of heart that refuses to let go of hope, the disciples remain clueless, thus confirming in their very obtuseness the great darkness in which we all share. Happily, Jesus will soon put an end to such nonsense.

➤ All-powerful Father, you who sent your Son
to those who have fallen asleep in sin,
grant us the grace to receive this healing Word
and so awaken to a life that will never end.

CHAPTER 5

Jesus the Ever-Greater Good

Then Jesus told [his disciples] plainly, "Lazarus is dead; and for your sake I am glad that I was not there, so that you may believe. But let us go to him." Thomas, called the Twin, said to his fellow disciples, "Let us also go, that we may die with him."

—Jn 11:14–16

A demand both unexpected and impertinent was once put to Henry James, whom keepers of the literary tablets regard as among the greatest storytellers of the last century: "Do tell me what you think of life." Without missing a beat, he answered, "I think it is a predicament which precedes death."[1]

---

1. Martin Cyril D'Arcy, *Death and Life* (New York: Longmans, Green & Co, 1948), p. vii.

Years later, stretched out upon his own deathbed, there to confront the dread finality itself, he greeted it thus: "So here it is at last, the distinguished thing!"[2] One wonders, seeing that final *turn of the screw*, what sort of tale might he have then told.

But back to Lazarus, whose own story we've been following right along from the pages of John's Gospel. And, straightaway, it occurs that the predicament he's been having is an altogether unique one. In fact, he will shortly fail to survive it, which is why the poor fellow has been pronounced quite definitively dead. But is he *really* dead? Because Jesus, no sooner having announced the news of his passing to the disciples, is determined to go to him, in order, as he told them earlier, "to awaken him." How does that work? And why now? For what purpose? I mean, if Christ had only gone to him sooner—around the time, say, he'd first been importuned by a couple of distraught sisters—his friend might well have been spared the frightful experience of actually having to die.

---

2. From Edith Wharton, who had been James' great friend, who recalled it in her book, *A Backward Glance* (New York: D. Appleton Century, 1934), p. 409.

So why the added torment? Was it really necessary to have to put him through it? What is death, anyway? And what does it mean for Lazarus to die? It surely cannot mean less than the most fearful ordeal. It is not an experience of achievement, in other words, like moving up the ladder of success; but rather of disintegration, of a final fall into the abyss of a common and universal predicament. In the face of death we dare not sentimentalize, for it is as relentless an enemy as it is repugnant; indeed, a harrowing of all that we have, all that we know. It is no less than a complete sundering of body from soul, the prospect of which can only plunge us into a state of deepest horror and dismay.

Up against so awful a finality, our resources are strictly limited. We draw upon such weaponry as we have. The written word, for instance, especially in its imaginative rearrangement of the raw data of death, which may succeed in rendering the experience in a particularly vivid way, thus enabling the reader to see what the poet Webster called "the skull beneath the skin." The French novelist François Mauriac, for instance, in describing a young man entering a room where his father, freshly dead, awaits entombment, draws the reader emotionally into the boy's fear, his dread. We see him "tremble all over like a sapling," before the fact of death, and we too feel the tremor "of the death that lies deep down in all of us, ready to take charge, the one indubitable truth, the only certainty."

Mauriac gives his character a voice to ask these questions. "What was the point," the young man wants to know,

> of reading newspapers? How could anything in the world matter when death was the sentence under which it lay? *That* news emptied all other news of meaning. Why strive to learn, when tomorrow one would be cast forth as refuse, rotting and decayed? The only truth. . . . If there exists anything beyond, we do not know it. We can be sure only of death.[3]

If it be true, then, as Mauriac insists, that only stones are spared the fate of having to die, then it makes sense that Christ would tell his disciples how glad he was for their sake that he and they were not there to see Lazarus die. Not because their nerves were of such

---

3. *The Unknown Sea* (New York: Penguin, 1962), pp. 43–44.

delicacy that the sight of a dead man would unnerve them, but because, for all of us, the sheer datum of death is not to be borne by any man.

Here are matters which, as Pascal would say, take us all by the throat. They especially turn, in a Christian context, on the question of faith, of which the disciples appear to have little to show. Nor have we, actually. It was precisely for the gift of that faith that Jesus had put off going to Lazarus in the first place. But in going now, Jesus, armed with the very weaponry of God himself, is able all the more convincingly to demonstrate his capacity to destroy death. Will this move them to place their trust in him? To surrender their own futures to him? Because, like children, they first need to see in order to believe. And if Lazarus had been prevented from dying, which is the usual and wholly predictable result of a life tending toward death, because Jesus was already there, how would they ever know that he had the power to break the kingdom of death in two?

Of course, they understand nothing of this. Constrained to see things in earthly terms only, they would sooner force the Lord of the universe onto a Procrustean bed, in which the always-greater aspect of divine mystery disappears altogether, than to submit in a kind of nakedness of faith to the designs of a God beyond their capacity to know. Or desire. St. Thérèse of Lisieux, the sweep of whose own desire was given boundless expression even amid the shades of prolonged suffering—which could not dim the "always more" aspect of her hope—reminds us that "we can never have too much trust in our dear God, who is so powerful and so merciful." Indeed, she tells us, sounding repeatedly the depths of her heavenly hope, "One receives as much from him as one hopes for."

How far are we willing to venture? Are we like those who, never expecting too much from God, deliberately downsize our demands so that we ask only what we think God capable of giving, which (alas) is not much? How far we've fallen from the childlike confidence of Thérèse, who, referencing God and his saints, announces that "they are waiting to see how far I will go in my trust," then adding, "but not in vain was my heart pierced by that saying of Job's: 'Even if you kill me, I will have hope in you.'"[4]

---

4. Quotes here and in the previous paragraph taken from Hans Urs von Balthasar, *Dare We Hope "That All Men Be Saved"?*, trans. David Kipp and Lothar Krauth (San Francisco: Ignatius, 1988), pp. 102–103.

God is not the least bit like us. And if we were to measure out his mercies with coffee spoons, or try and fit them into a teacup, he would at once cease to be God. We must, as St. Anselm tells us, along with the entire Patristic tradition on which he stands, see most clearly that we do not see. If you will insist on knowing the ways of God, then it is not God whom you know.

This is why, in the circumstance of raising Lazarus from the dead, Jesus will need to stretch his disciples so that, while he forever exceeds their reach, they may yet come round to the conclusion that here is an ever-greater God whose mysteries are worth every effort to grasp.

✦ Loving Father, in sending your Son to Lazarus
  our brother, we glimpse the always-greater glory
  of your Mystery. Enlarge our faith so that,
  like Lazarus, we too may recognize the signs
  of your coming among us.

CHAPTER 6

Giving Death
Its Due

Now when Jesus came, he found that Lazarus had already been in the tomb four days. Bethany was near Jerusalem, about two miles off, and many of the Jews had come to Martha and Mary to console them concerning their brother.

—Jn 11: 17–19

I once knew a fellow who, anytime he was asked how he was doing, would invariably reply, "I am decomposing." The odd thing was that he lived a very long and healthy life, pegging out at around ninety or so. Perhaps it was hyperbole that finally killed him.

Nevertheless, the point survives his exaggeration of it. We are all decomposing. Despite ever more frantic and ingenious attempts to shore up the sagging flesh, decline and death take no holiday. None of us are safe from such depredations when, from womb to tomb, we remain fixed objects of their pursuit. Not even the most imaginative of cosmetic reconstructions can keep these beasts at bay. Efforts to reverse the aging process are not only hopeless, but quite imbecilic. Mortality will forever be getting in the way. We are, it would seem, born to die. To quote that old blues tune,

> You may be beautiful,
> But you gonna die someday,
> So how's about a little lovin'
> Before you pass away."[1]

While the lyric may not exactly equal Gerard Manley Hopkins, whose wonderfully evocative title, "That Nature Is a Heraclitean Fire and On the Comfort of the Resurrection," reminds us that "Flesh fade and mortal trash / Fall to the residuary worm," the conclusion is no different. Namely, the brute certainty that in the end we are all fated to die. "Man," Hopkins laments, "how fast his fire dint, his mark on mind, is

---

1. Big Joe Turner and Pete Johnson, "Roll 'Em Pete" (Vocalion 4607, 1938).

gone!" How soon the ax falls, in other words, sending us into the same common and bloody ditch. "Death blots black out; nor mark / Is any of him at all so stark / But vastness blurs and time beats level."[2]

Life is no picnic, in other words. Or, if it is, the irony of the outcome is more likely to resemble *Picnic at Hanging Rock* than sandwiches and tea on the back porch. That was, by the way, a darkly sinister movie, made in Australia some years ago, in which a bevy of boarding school girls bound for a picnic vanishes into thin air, their disappearance to this day an unsolved mystery. Like ashes blown out to sea, they never return.

In short, nobody gets out alive, the Old Guy having seen to that. Not since the time of Adam and Eve, at least, who, thanks to the seductions of sin, got themselves thrown out of a garden that was once a paradise—leaving them to face, as the poet Milton tells us, "a long day's dying to augment their pain."[3]

The point is, we are all falling, like so many hapless bodies consigned to the earth. "This hand falls," writes

---

2. Gerard Manley Hopkins, "That Nature is a Heraclitean Fire and of the comfort of the Resurrection," *Poems of Gerard Manley Hopkins*, ed. Robert Bridges (London: Humphrey Milford, 1918).

3. *Paradise Lost* (Glasgow: Robert and Andrew Foulis, 1776), X.

Rainer Maria Rilke in his poem "Autumn." "And look at others: It is in them all."[4] And, once again, the awful unraveling that leads to the great nightfall that will leave us all bereft, begins very early on. Indeed, from the first moment we've begun to be, we are old enough to die. The instant we've left the starting block, heading for the light, darkness hovers about us, threatening at every turn to prevent our seeing it. Life becomes no more than a movement towards death, an expiration date stamped upon every birth. The flesh fairly crawls contemplating stuff like that.

Or even seeing pious pictures of the child Jesus gently laid upon Our Lady's lap:

In swaddling clothes she wraps the Child,

Against the unseen outline of a shroud.

Darkest omen of approaching cloud.

And how the tears will accompany both events, whether it be birth or, at an interval which is seldom decent, death, the final cancellation, as it were, which we carry always before us.

---

4. Rainer Maria Rilke, "Autumn," *Translations from the Poetry of Rainer Maria Rilke*, trans. M. D. Herter Norton (New York: W. W. Norton & Company, Inc., 1938), p. 75.

Then, of course, there is Shakespeare, on whom nothing mortal was ever lost. In *Measure for Measure*,[5] he gives us the noble Claudio, whose first impulse is to forfeit his own life to save a beloved sister. How it endears him to us. "If I must die," he announces bravely, "I will encounter darkness as a bride, / And hug it in my arms." But so unnerved is he by the thought of actual death, the poor man will at once importune his sister to forfeit *her* virtue for his life! In a speech fraught with all the horror we associate with death, he declares:

Ay, but to die, and go we know not where,
To lie in cold obstruction and to rot,
This sensible warm motion to become.
A kneaded clod; and the delighted spirit
To bathe in fiery floods, or to reside.
In thrilling region of thick-ribbed ice;
To be imprisoned in the viewless winds,
And blown with restless violence round about
The pendent world; or to be worse than worst.
Of those that lawless and incertain thought.

5. Act 3, scene 1.

Imagine howling—'tis too horrible!
The weariest and most loathed worldly life
That age, ache, penury, and imprisonment
Can lay on nature is a paradise.
To what we fear of death.

It is no surprise, therefore, when Jesus arrives four days after the body of Lazarus had first entered the tomb, that the course of its corruption has taken matters well in hand. Signs of decay are not easily disguised in a desert land. As an obvious biological datum, the decomposing body is not a pretty sight. And the smell is worse. The situation, in other words, looks entirely hopeless. Perhaps this is why so many of his friends and neighbors have come round to offer the usual bromides; these, of course, will prove especially hollow since there is really no comfort to give. The dead have a way of staying dead.

But the real reason that their presence proves so inane and feckless is that it is not they, but Christ, the Lord of History and the Cosmos, who can bring a consolation that is both genuine and lasting—because it truly transforms the situation. Only he may take sorrow in hand and turn it all to joy. Yet, by their merely being there, the friends of the dead man will provide a necessary witness to the miracle that Jesus has come to perform. Death can lay no claim on the one who in fact came into the world to lift its curse, ensuring for us that the sting of death shall leave no lasting hurt.

➤ All-powerful and ever-living Father, death can lay no claim on you. Grant, we beseech you, the grace to overcome the oppressions of our mortality, and thus lift the curse of death forever.

CHAPTER 7

Martha's Moxie

When Martha heard that Jesus was coming, she went to meet him, while Mary sat in the house. Martha said to Jesus, "Lord, if you had been here, my brother would not have died. [But] even now I know that whatever you ask of God, God will give you."

—Jn 11:20–22

I t is said that there are three kinds of people in the world. There are those who make things happen. Those who watch things happen. And, finally, those who wonder what happened. At the end of the day, nothing ever happens to them, they simply shuffle off to the grave, the world having received no impression whatsoever from their leaving it. Meanwhile, their souls are sent to the Nether World where, Dante tells us, they fall in with the futile, whose ranks are swollen with the paltry and the pathetic, those countless small-minded souls who proved themselves equally odious to both God and the devil. "Heaven cast them forth," he tells us in Canto 3 of the *Inferno*, "their presence there would dim the light; / Deep Hell rejects so base a herd, / Lest sin should boast itself because of them."

Not nearly good enough to go to Hell, you see, they haven't the least hunger for heaven either. In life they stood for nothing; nor did they ever stand against anything. They simply sat on the fence, moving neither up nor down. "They made no waves," says Dante, "and so they made no name." Joined thus forever, he adds, "to that self-seeking squad / Of angels fitted neither to rebel / Against, nor put their heartfelt faith in God."[1] So vast is their number, Dante tells us in a line so lapidary that T. S. Eliot will lift it for his own use in "The Waste Land," "I had not thought death had undone so many."[2]

Where exactly are they, then, in the scheme of the underworld? Dante, in an exercise of condign justice, sticks them in a sort of suburb of Hell, called the Vestibule, where they are condemned to suffer forever, shorn

---

1. See his *Inferno*, Canto 3.

2. T. S. Eliot, "The Waste Land," *The Waste Land: A Facsimile and Transcript of the Original Drafts Including the Annotations of Ezra Pound*, ed. Valerie Eliot (Orlando, Fla.: Harcourt, Inc., 1971), section I, line 62.

of both mercy and remembrance. And why is that? Because, in the end, not to choose is to choose, it is to throw in one's lot with all the other shades of indecision. For their state is grievous indeed. Enough certainly to forfeit what every ancient moralist from Aristotle to the authors of the New Testament have called "the good of the intellect," which is God himself. And, of course, to know and to love God is what brings salvation. Miss Dorothy Sayers, in her superb commentary on Dante's *Divine Comedy*, explains it this way:

> Heaven and Hell being states in which choice is permanently fixed, there must also be a state in which the refusal of choice is itself fixed, since to refuse choice is in fact to choose indecision. The Vestibule is the abode of the weather-cock mind, the vague tolerance which will neither approve nor condemn, the cautious cowardice for which no decision is ever final.[3]

Has there ever been a better description of the Catholic pro-choice politician? How exquisitely precise the

---

3. Dorothy L. Sayers, trans., Dante Alighieri, *Inferno*, in *The Comedy of Dante Alighieri, the Florentine*, vol. 1 (New York: Penguin, 1949), p. 89.

fate of those wretched souls, therefore, sunk beneath the impacted weight of a lifetime's indecision! "What the lost souls have lost," she asserts, "is not the intellect itself, which still functions mechanically, but the *good* of the intellect, i.e., the knowledge of God, who is Truth."[4]

Which brings us back in a seemingly circuitous way to dear, practical Martha, whom we need now to usher onto the stage. Such an amazing woman she was, who certainly did not lose the good of *her* intellect. The ever-practical, always alert, and active sister of Lazarus, her supply of moxie seems never to have run out. She was not one of those who wonder what happened. Whatever needed to be done, she was immediately on board to do it. Her kind are the sensible ones who make things happen, whether it's food or a fuss. And so, ever redoubtable, she does not hesitate an instant in going out to meet Jesus on the road, there to accost him about doing something which, in her brisk and businesslike way, he could so easily have done before. "Lord," she says, addressing him in an abrupt and indeed accusatory tone, "if you had been here, my brother would not have died."

---

4. Sayers, trans., *Inferno*, p. 90.

And isn't that a quite stunning admission of faith! Indeed, here is an example of confidence of which no expression more resolute or robust can be imagined. But, pray, how does she know this about Jesus? Not even the prayerful Mary, presumably left woolgathering while stout Martha is launching her salient, would dare venture to speak thus to the Lord. And so, apart from the usual immortal longings that spring eternal from the human heart, why does she do it? What has moved her to put everything on the line?

The answer, of course, is she does not know. Which is why, not to put too fine a point on the matter, hope and knowledge are not the same thing, and that it would be most unwise to confuse the two. I can puzzle out the sum of two plus two, and know with sheer apodictic certitude the outcome will absolutely be four. But the outcome of my life? Please. I cannot know the answer to that question, even as I persist in the most lively hope that it will turn out well. In telling us that "all shall be well and all manner of things shall be well,"[5] the Lady Julian of Norwich was not speaking as

---

5. Julian of Norwich, *Revelations of Divine Love*, ed. Grace Warrack (London: Methuen & Co., 1901), chap. 27, p. 56.

a mathematician, but as a mystic. The sixteen *Shewings* God favored her with were not an exercise in geometry, but grace.

What, then, is hope but Peguy's "little girl," who greets us each morning with a spring in her step, blithely expecting only good things from the God who loves her. It is "the thing with feathers," to quote that wonderful nineteenth-century wit, the bafflingly reclusive Emily Dickinson, "that perches in the soul - / And sings the tune without the words - / And never stops - at all -."[6]

Yes, Martha is armed and fortified by hope as we all know and have it. But with her there is more. While it was not any sort of empirically grounded knowledge that moved her, it was nevertheless a most adamantine sense of trust, a profound certainty that God would grant Jesus all he asks, which fiercely informed her conviction that, "even now," it would be possible to bring her brother back. Not for a moment does she doubt either the capacity of Christ to do this, nor his willingness to undertake so dramatic a rescue mission for the sake of someone they both love.

---

6. Emily Dickinson, "'Hope' is the Thing with Feathers - (314)," *The Complete Poems of Emily Dickinson*, ed. Thomas H. Johnson (Cambridge, Mass.: Harvard University Press, 1951).

If he wishes to retrieve her lost brother from the dark grave of death, then let him get on with it. Here is an intimation of real hope, theologically understood, that Christ came into the world to give to us all. The kind of hope, moreover, whose outcome does not depend on us. For if it did, then that would be to place it within the reach of ourselves, not God. Who as Father of us all, including his own Son, will not refuse us anything.

➤ Father in heaven, give us the grace to be like Martha, and thus to persist always in the loving certainty that nothing is impossible for those who entrust themselves to you.

CHAPTER 8

Resurrection Is Real

Jesus said to [Martha], "Your brother will rise again." Martha said to him, "I know that he will rise again in the resurrection at the last day." Jesus said to her, "I am the resurrection and the life; he who believes in me, though he die, yet shall he live, and whoever lives and believes in me shall never die. Do you believe this?"

—Jn 11:23–26

Of all creatures great and small, man alone knows that he must fall. And that death, the last rung on the ladder of mortality, awaits us in the end. "He's the ruffian on the stair," writes the poet W. E. Henley. You know, that thuggish looking fellow, "with his knee-bones at your chest, / And his knuckles in your throat."[1] Who has not, by the way, come to take your coat. But

---

1. William Ernest Henley, "Madam Life's a Piece in Bloom," *Poems* (London: Macmillan and Co., 1920), p. 87.

to snatch you violently away. So you might just as well go quietly as he'll have you in the end anyway. Or, to lend the scene a slightly more fastidious air, a courtly old gentleman come to impart news no one wants to hear, as witness the unwelcome fellow in a quietly devastating poem by John Crowe Ransom called "Piazza Piece."[2] Introducing himself to the lovely young lady as "a gentleman in a dustcoat," he endeavors without success to engage her in conversation. Something portentous is on his mind but, alas, she does not wish to hear it. "Your ears are soft and small," he says,

> And listen to an old man not at all,
> They want the young men's whispering
>   and sighing.
> But see the roses on your trellis dying
> And hear the spectral singing of the moon;
> For I must have my lovely lady soon,
> I am a gentleman in a dustcoat trying.

Neither trellis nor rose can last forever, and even the loveliest among us is fated to die, signed with an expiration date of which so many remain blithely

---

2. See his *Poems and Essays*, (New York: Random House, 1955), p. 38.

unaware. Until, that is, the ruffian arrives, leaving us no exit except the waiting grave. On that day death will have set his trap, and there are no blandishments by which the beautiful, or the clever, or even the good, may undo the spring. "Alone of gods," Aeschylus tells us,

> Death has no love for gifts,
> Libation helps you not, nor sacrifice.
> He has no altar, and he hears no hymns;
> From him alone Persuasion stands apart."[3]

What will happen to those we love when it is their turn to die? When the outward shell of the self we rejoiced so recently to know and to love is lowered into the ground? Husbands and wives, mothers and fathers, the children we once knew, grown and scattered into the wind. Where do they all go when they are gone? And why must they go at all?

"The houses are all gone under the sea," writes T. S. Eliot, hitting the right elegiac note. "The dancers are all gone under the hill":

---

3. From his play *Niobe*, whose titular character the gods punished after hearing her boast of her many children—all of whom were destroyed.

O dark dark dark. They all go into the dark

[. . .]

The captains, merchant bankers, eminent men
  of letters,

The generous patrons of art, the statesmen and
  the rulers,

Distinguished civil servants, chairmen of many
  committees,

Industrial lords and petty contractors, all go into
  the dark

[. . .]

And we all go with them, in the silent funeral.[4]

Once again, when it comes to death and dying,
there are no exceptions; we shall all be required by the
cruelty of a common fate to leave everything behind.
Indeed, we each know, however long or pleasant the
play, that the last act will prove bloody. None of us is
exempt from that final curtain call, through the silence
of which we shall all someday pass. Alone. We shall
pass through the door of death, which admits only

---

4. T. S. Eliot, "East Coker," *Four Quartets* (New York: Harcourt, Brace, 1943), section II, lines 278–279; section III, lines 280, 282–285, 289.

one at a time, and we'll all have been scheduled to go through it. All the golden lads and girls, the chimney sweeps as well, unto the same dust. "Roses have thorns, and silver fountains mud," says Shakespeare. "Clouds and eclipses stain both moon and sun, / And loathsome canker lives in sweetest bud."[5] Yes, for all of us, the bright day will soon be done, we'll go down with the setting sun.

But suppose that to happen to God himself, that he should descend, albeit freely, into those same dark "interstellar spaces, the vacant into the vacant"? What then? How vastly different death would then be! To the dead, certainly. And what about the living who, with stabbing and persistent loss, mourn their passing? Like the family and friends of Lazarus, whose fate is to mourn the one they love? Forced thus to bear the pain of his absence, what recourse have they? Even if they, fellow mortals, were to follow him into those deep cavernous regions where the dead must dwell—there "to lie in cold obstruction,"[6] as Shakespeare tells us—it would do them no good. Certainly, it would make no difference for poor Lazarus.

---

5. Taken from his Sonnet 35.

6. *Measure for Measure*, act 3, scene 1.

We are all like Orpheus, you see, that mythic figure in desperate search of Eurydice, his young bride, lost to him on the day of their wedding, for whom the gods so arrange matters that he might return from that awful place with her in tow, provided he does not look back as she climbs safely out. But, alas, he does, thus losing her forever. For all the loveliness of his music—so beguiling, we are told, "he drew iron tears down Pluto's cheek, / and made Hell itself grant what Love did seek"[7]—could not finally ensure the safety of his bride.

Yes, but Orpheus is not God, who, unlike things mortal, remains free, blessedly and powerfully so, to reach into the darkness and bring them all back. "Your brother will rise," Jesus tells Martha, a declaration followed by that astonishing, heart-stopping affirmation revealing the absolute uniqueness of the Christian claim: "I am the resurrection and the life; whoever believes in me, even if he dies, will live, and everyone who lives and believes in me will never die."

How does one improve upon that? Isn't that the music we most long to hear? The tocsin whose sound

---

7. While the myth itself is credited to Virgil and Ovid, these poetic lines are from John Milton, "Il Penseroso," *Poems Upon Several Occasions*, ed. Thomas Warton (London: James Dodsley, 1785), p. 81, lines 105–108.

is sweeter than life itself, because it is the source of life? "[B]efore Abraham was, I am" (Jn 8:58), says Jesus, to the astonishment of the world. And isn't the realm of the dead the very place where the chord of hope is struck with an absolute majestic finality? "One short sleep past," the poet Donne reports, "we wake eternally; / And death shall be no more; death thou shalt die."[8] It is a song that only Christ can sing, which means that without the tuning fork of faith, which the Church as conductor holds trustfully in her hands, our ears will not be attuned to hear it.

➛ All powerful God and Father,
you are the true giver of life.
Keep us safe in your Son's keeping,
whom you sent into Sheol
to bring the dead back to life.

8. See his Sonnet 10.

CHAPTER 9

The Promised One Has Come

[Martha] said to him, "Yes, Lord; I believe that you are the Christ, the Son of God, he who is coming into the world." When she had said this, she went and called her sister Mary, saying quietly, "The Teacher is here and is calling for you."

—Jn 11:27–28

On hearing the news from Jesus' own lips that her brother Lazarus shall certainly rise again—which is, admittedly, a most astonishing, horizon-shattering announcement—how does Martha react? More to the point, what does she then say when Jesus flat out tells her, "*I am the resurrection and the life*," and that "*whoever lives and believes in me shall never die*"? Because, dear reader, that is *the* game changer. And make no mistake, whatever she says, it will have come from a place of wonderment and stupefaction unimaginably profound. Indeed, in words every bit as marvelous and amazing as the event which has prompted her to say them.

"Yes, Lord, I have come to believe that you are the Messiah, the Son of God, the one who is coming into the world."

At that very moment and in that precise place, never mind how unwittingly she may have stumbled upon it, Martha has declared the deepest possible truth of the human heart. That here we have the highest human desire of all, the one which most profoundly and insistently defines who we are and why we exist. Namely the desire for God, for the everlasting life that he has come into the world to give us. What other longing is there? It is the bedrock truth about us, a fact so fundamental to who we are that, alone among all the other truths, it qualifies as *the* constitutive and defining datum of our humanity. We are made for God alone and thus we can only be, only exist, in relation to him. There can be no other end to which we were born to strive, no greater or more consuming good to which we could possibly be drawn, than life with him.

"I am my beloved's and my beloved is mine" (Song 6:3). Life could never get any better than this. Because, once again, there is no other thing for which we aspire with equal or unending thirst. And even were we sinfully to suppress the desire, it would not go away. It's the life for which we were made, a life with God that can never fade. No single created thing for which an appetite exists, or longing for which we pine, could conceivably correspond to the joys that await us on the other side of death. An eternity of bliss, no less, spent in the arms of almighty God, in whom every blessed angel and saint shall find rest. Against a backdrop like that, there is no competition.

"What the soul hardly realizes," Dom Hubert Van Zeller tells us, "is that unbeliever or not, his loneliness is really a homesickness for God."[1] In fact, in a Chestertonian image that pushes the envelope as far as it will go, even were the sinner to pound haplessly away on the door of a brothel, he would still be looking for God. In the worst possible place, to be sure; nevertheless, even for him,

---

1. From *Suffering in Other Words: A Presentation for Beginners* (Springfield, Ind.: Templegate, 1964).

the most abject of sinners, salvation may only be five minutes away.[2]

Behold the mystery of *imago Dei*, the spiritual creature formed by God in his own image, in order to become the very likeness thereof. Why else would God, the Infinite Other, wish to fashion us finite beings unless it were to answer a need, to direct a drive, a dynamism, already rooted and thus determinative of what it means to be human? And it is Christ, of course, who will be orchestrating this drive. How beautifully Hopkins puts it in one of his untitled fragments:

> Thee God, I come from, to thee go,
> All day long I like fountain flow.
> From thy hand out, swayed about.
> Mote-like in thy mighty glow.[3]

If that, then, is the idea of man on which we are to build, what shall we call God's answering response

---

2. As much as one would wish to assign this to Chesterton, it may well have first surfaced in Bruce Marshall's novel *All Glorious Within* (also published as *The World, The Flesh, and Father Smith*) (London: Constable & Co, 1944), p. 124.

3. Gerard Manley Hopkins, 'Thee, God, I come from, to thee go,' *Poems*, ed. Robert Bridges (London: Humphrey Milford, 1918), poem no. 73.

but an event of revelation no greater than which can be imagined? In what does it consist but the sending of his Son, who, in breaking himself to become our bread, beckons us to a life of eternal love and communion. Think of it. The uncreated Word entering into our fallen world, becoming one of us in his daring descent to the very bottom of our brokenness, determined thereby to set everything straight. "There is no tale ever told," exulted J. R. R. Tolkien, "that men would rather find was true, and none which so many sceptical men have accepted as true on its own merits."[4]

What a nice touch, too, in having the sensible and practical-minded Martha be among the very first to strike the chord, the mystic chord, that carries the sound of his music. Scripture has given her, without a doubt, one of the best lines in the Gospel. It enables her to pay Jesus the highest possible compliment, which is her stunning admission that he is in fact the Christ, the Anointed One from above.

Leaving aside the world of first century Palestine, which must still make up its mind about him, it goes

---

4. J. R. R. Tolkien, "On Fairy-tales," in *The Monsters and the Critics, and Other Essays*, ed. Christopher Reuel Tolkien (London: Allen and Unwin, 1983), p. 156.

without saying that he at least has no doubts on that score. He knows himself to be the Messiah. There is not any of that cringing uncertainty about who he is or why he has come. Concerning his identity and his mission, Christ is refreshingly clear and uncompromisingly robust. None of that demythologizing nonsense of which one finds only too many examples in modern theology—when God himself must, as Kierkegaard cleverly opines, "wait in the lobby while the scholars upstairs debate his existence."[5]

But because Jesus wishes others to come to an acknowledgement of his divine standing, it pleases him to hear Martha say it. "Yes, Lord . . . you are the Messiah . . . the one who is coming into the world." Our world, that is, the turning world, where, all at once and in the concrete particulars of Palestine, *the still point* happens, turning everything on its head for the first time. And as it radiates its blessed presence out into the four winds, we are privileged to watch. "A split second," says Rita Simmonds in a lovely little poem, "an instant / the flash of an angel's wing." And in that instant, she tells us,

---

5. *The Present Age* (New York: Harper & Row, 1962), p. 148.

The whole world changed . . . imperceptibly
radically
different
and from that moment on
Eternity came
and has forever stayed
maternally entwined
in time."[6]

So, how does Martha know all this? The answer
is the grace of God, which alone may account for all
our certainties of belief. Faith is the enabling gift.
And faith, as von Balthasar tells us, "is the surrender
of the finite person in his entirety to the infinite person."[7] It is, paradoxically, the most powerful weapon
the creature has, this ability to surrender, to say yes
to God. And what other surrender is worth making if
not this? An act of total self-giving to God, thereupon
unleashing a power greater than all the atom bombs
in the world. There is yet more: a total submission

---

6. Rita Simmonds, "Word Made Flesh," *Magnificat Year of Faith Com-panion*, Oct 11, 2012 to Nov 24, 2013, p. 195.

7. *Word and Redemption* (New York: Herder and Herder, 1965), p. 8.

of love, which, in the order of time, as von Balthasar goes on to tell us, "reveals itself as hope," thus joining each of the three virtues into a single uninterrupted mosaic of divine grace.

And, finally, where does Martha go with the faith and the love and the hope that now animate her heart, moving right down to the bottom of her being? Why, she goes off to fetch her sister Mary, letting her know that Jesus is here, "asking for you." Such is the office of those in the active life: to go and alert the contemplatives to attend to the loftiest pursuit of all, communion with the Lord. Her sister will be grateful for the summons.

➤ All-merciful and loving Father, in giving us the God-man to be our Redeemer, you delivered on your promise to set us free. We praise and glorify you for your surpassing goodness.

CHAPTER 10

Longing for God

And when [Mary] heard it, she rose quickly and went to [Jesus]. Now Jesus had not yet come to the village, but was still in the place where Martha had met him. When the Jews who were with her in the house, consoling her, saw Mary rise quickly and go out, they followed her, supposing that she was going to the tomb to weep there.

—Jn 11:29–31

Years ago I came across this charming anecdote, probably made-up (and no doubt some pedant will shortly prove it), but I'd like to think it was Oscar Wilde who, on first seeing Niagara Falls, pronounced it an almost perfect prodigy of nature—provided one slight improvement were made in the direction of the flow of water. Arrange it to move upwards, he proposed, rather than allowing it, in the usual boring and predictable way, to fall downwards. Only then would its perfection be complete.

What a delightful confirmation of the Principle of Tropism! And what is that but the tendency of all living things to long for the light, and so stretch themselves in the direction of its source. Like the explanation I once heard about why bananas are bent. It's because they grow against the grain of gravity, their resistance to which causing them to curve while straining skyward. Sounds quaint but, as we've so often been instructed in the past year, just follow the science.

Turning to another and superior science, however, which is theology, St. Augustine teaches that if it be true that love is a kind of gravitational pull, drawing the soul upwards to God, the true *Helios*, which happens in the order of grace, then why shouldn't we, in the order of nature, witness in water an analogous avidity for light, rising towards the natural sun? A longing to return, in other words, to its own source, the point of its ultimate origin, to wit, the great burning ball in the heavens whence life on planet earth begins. Isn't that why sunflowers grow so tall?

And mightn't this be why crushed grapes, when quickened by a process called fermentation, eventually transmute into a quite delicious burgundy? In fact, on looking into the miracle at Cana, it was Saint Augustine who, for all that he did not know about the science of fermentation, nevertheless suggested that it wasn't because Christ had merely suspended the laws of nature that produced an abundance of wonderful wine. It was rather an intensification, a dramatic speeding up of a process which, in his naïveté, he imagined would quite naturally occur in any case. He was, of course, mistaken in his assumption that water alone would serve as the catalyst, but since Christ clearly drew huge quantities of wine from water it surely represents a most apt symbol of the entire sacramental system, one in which grace is forever building upon nature. And, come to think of it, it was Aquinas, the Common Doctor, who, centuries later when accosted by his enemies for "watering down" the pure gospel by baptizing Aristotle, answered their objection by directly appealing to Cana. "I too," he assured them, "am transforming water into wine!"[1]

---

1. To paraphrase a quote found in Norman Kretzmann and Eleonore Stump (eds.), *The Cambridge Companion to Aquinas* (Cambridge: Cambridge University Press, 1993), p. 235.

The principle, therefore, which set like gothic stone in the period of High Scholasticism, was this: *Gratia supponit et perficit naturam*, which means that grace builds upon and perfects nature. Which brings me to all those pilgrims and tourists who travel to Rome. Included in their itinerary is often a visit to the Pantheon, which is among the glories of the ancient world, a vivid testimony both to the architecture and the piety of pre-Christian peoples. There is something odd about it, however, which is that there's a blooming hole in the ceiling, stretching 142 feet into the air. So high is it that, not infrequently, when it rains it will not quite reach ground zero, having more or less evaporated on the way down.

Well, why is that? The answer is not the least bit odd inasmuch as the whole point of the place was to provide a setting for the worship of the pagan gods, access to which took place thanks to the hole in the roof. I mean, what better way to allow for the sheer verticality of human desire than a building the blueprints for which include a large opening onto the realm of the gods?

After all, it is the thirst for God, for the whole world of the numinous, that draws the spirit upward, its yearning finally to be free of the limitations of space and time. Not to try and breach such barriers as stand in the way of transcendence, in effect closing off the ceiling that connects earth with the heavens, would be a terrible injustice. Even pagans are entitled to chase after their dreams, scanning the night sky for signs of the divine. Why not, in the circumstance, leave open a space to permit free and unfettered worship of the Mystery? Especially as it answers so deep and primordial a desire for God.

"If nature has placed within me an impulse," as Luigi Giussani puts it in *The Religious Sense*, "even more powerful than a rocket, a drive so deeply rooted that it actually constitutes my very self, then why must the answer to the question generated by this impulse represent a goal so impossible that it is useless to speak of it?"[2] The question, *What is the meaning of everything?* which provides the very scaffolding of the religious sense, is not something only misfits ask. It is an absolute, universal, necessary question; the most compelling question any human being could possibly ask. Not

---

2. *The Religious Sense*, trans. John Zucchi (London: McGill-Queen's University Press, 1997), p. 61.

to ask it, indeed, to organize one's life without continuing reference to it, is a sign of an illness far worse than anything medicine might identify, much less remedy. It is a disease of the spirit.

Not even the state, equipped with its vaunted machinery of power, can put an end to the desire for God. "Against the wild prayer of longing," declares W. H. Auden, "legislation remains helpless."[3] When the historian Tacitus, who chronicled the greatness of Rome, asked himself what made it so, he did not cite the size or strength of its army, nor the nobility of its rulers, but rather the temples of its gods.

Perhaps now is a good time to put in a word for the Principle of *Theo*-tropism, and so confirm the happy continuity between gravity and grace. Between, that is, nature's light, which is the sun, and that far greater light which is Christ, on whom the glory of the Father shines with a luster so incandescent that nothing can ever succeed in putting it out.

How fitting, then, that we should apply all this to Mary, sister of Lazarus, whose longing to be with the

---

3. From Herod's soliloquy found in W. H. Auden, "For the Time Being: A Christmas Oratorio," in *For the Time Being* (New York: Random House, 1944).

Lord is so ardent and uncomplicated that on hearing news of Jesus, she rises at once and goes immediately to him. Even before he arrives, she goes unhesitatingly to meet him. It is as if her thirst for God were so great, so consuming, that an intimation of the blessed presence had already made itself felt, filling her heart with the foretaste of waters more abundant even than those of the mighty falls along the Niagara; indeed, waters that will never run dry.

How like the character in the Flannery O'Connor story she is, whose hunger was so great, he said, that he could have eaten all the loaves and the fishes after Jesus had multiplied them.[4] Or Catherine of Siena, who, early on in her mystical journey to God, made the happy discovery that, as she tells the rest of us, those whose shoe size is far from mystical, "All the way to Heaven, is Heaven, because Christ is the Way."

➛ Heavenly Father, source of life-giving waters,
we ask you to lead us always to springs that
will never run dry.

---

4. See her novel *The Violent Bear It Away* (New York: Farrar, Strauss and Giroux, 1960).

CHAPTER 11

Troubled by Her Tears

Then Mary, when she came where Jesus was and saw him, fell at his feet, saying to him, "Lord, if you had been here, my brother would not have died." When Jesus saw her weeping, and the Jews who came with her also weeping, he was deeply moved in spirit and troubled.

—Jn 11:32–33

It cannot be the case, not in this world certainly, that our words, which are necessarily finite and contingent, and therefore imperfect, will ever correspond to God's own Word, even as it is spoken to us through the mediation of words hallowed by their canonical appearance in Holy Scripture. There we encounter the language of the Holy Ghost, that sacredly terrifying discourse of God himself, delivered unto the Bride in whom Christ joined heaven and earth. The perfect wedding, as it were, first conceived in eternity, then consummated in time.

Every word, then, has got to count. Like Waterford Crystal, one cannot be too sparing. "A word is not the same with one writer as it is with another," wrote Charles Peguy in the last weeks of his life, which ended in violence along the Western Front in the first days of the Great War. "One tears it from his guts. The other pulls it out of his overcoat pocket."[1]

The words of the Fourth Gospel were not written down on scraps of paper plucked from the author's overcoat pocket. They were inspired by God himself, chiseled in cipher by the carpenter man himself, which is why they cannot be improved upon by anyone. Thus, in his account of Lazarus and the sisters who grieve over his death, John's words may be trusted, having already been tested by the plumb line of God's own Word. The reader believes him, therefore, when he describes the moment when Mary, falling at the feet of Jesus, speaks to him in a way which is by turns both

---

1. Charles Peguy, *Basic Verities: Prose and Poetry*, trans. Julien Green (New York: Pantheon Books, Inc., 1943).

accusation and supplication: "Lord, if you had been here, my brother would not have died."

But it is the action which follows that is truly startling, for Jesus, immediately upon hearing her cry of the heart, and seeing the tears as she openly weeps for the brother who is no more, appears himself to be moved with pity, actually becoming, as John describes the scene, "deeply moved in spirit and troubled." He is not indifferent to her pain, not clinically detached from the details as though so immured in his otherness that he need not take note of the choking sobs which reveal her anguish. "It is important," Pope Francis tells us, "that others make a breach in our hearts."[2] It matters, in other words, that when Christ calls those who mourn "blessed," and that "they shall be comforted," he is not only referring to others, but to himself as well. Otherwise, the attitude of compassion, of the willingness to suffer with and alongside those who suffer, has no meaning. It is an empty suit, the exercise of a technician only, and not that of "the wounded surgeon," of one who, as the poet Eliot writes,

---

2. General Audience, (December 2, 2020). Vatican website: *www.vatican.va.*

plies the steel that questions the distempered part
Beneath whose hands we feel the sharp compassion
  of the healer's art
Resolving the enigma of the fever chart.[3]

These are moving words indeed, reminding us that if one wishes healing and wholeness from the Father, which is the deepest driving desire of the human heart, that is, to find atonement (that is, *at-one-ment* with God, our neighbor, and ourselves), then it will not do to circumvent the Son in getting there. The quality of divine mercy, the pity that is without measure, can be seen only in the tears of the Son, who weeps for a world that has lost its way. For the Son is the only way to take us there, catapulting us into the arms of his Father. And while we may not know this with absolute arithmetic exactitude, nevertheless, as Augustine assures us, "we know that there must be something we do not know *towards which we feel driven*" (emphasis added).[4]

---

3. From "East Coker," Part IV.

4. From his Letter to Proba, a wealthy Roman widow, cited by Pope Benedict in his encyclical On Christian Hope *Spe Salvi* (November 30, 2007), no. 11. Vatican website, *www.vatican.va*.

Let's face it, among the human and earthly things we know, and pine to possess, there is nothing there that finally satisfies, that fills the hollowed-out space we carry along all our lives. We are left forever, as the poet Herbert expresses it, in a state of "repining restlessness,"[5] always longing for more. And we can no more abstain from wishing and hoping for this mysterious "something we do not know," than we can jump out of our skins. It is the flywheel that turns the engine of hope.

Which is why we dare not dispense with faith, either, since the two move most naturally in tandem. In fact, a synod of bishops some years ago issued a statement concerning the Church's faith under the rubric of "Our Hope"—thus situating the whole dynamism of faith in the perspective of hope. The Second Virtue, we call it, whose exercise awakens the little girl who, Peguy reminds us,[6] "rises every morning," a jaunty bounce in her step, eager to wish us all a bright and beautiful day. She is, says Peguy,

5. Herbert, "The Pulley," in *Herbert: Poems*.

6. Charles Peguy, "The Portal of the Mystery of Hope," in *The Portal of the Mystery of Hope*, trans. David Louis Schindler (London: Continuum, 2005).

the bloom, and the fruit, and the leaf, and the limb,
And the twig, and the shoot, and the seed,
   and the bud.
Hope is the shoot, and the bud of the bloom
Of eternity itself.

Leave out this middle virtue, he warns, along end-less roads leading to her older sisters, and you shall soon learn that

without her they wouldn't be anything.
But two women already grown old.
Two elderly women.
Wrinkled by life.
It's she, the little one, who carries them all.
Because Faith sees only what is.
But she, she sees what will be.
Charity loves only what is.
But she, she loves what will be.[7]

After all, what does being a Christian mean if not the recognition that in saying the Our Father, a prayer

---

7. From "The Portal of the Mystery of Hope."

which Jesus himself composed, in asking that "Thy Kingdom come," our petition is really about the end of an old and corrupt world, supplanted by the sudden breaking-in of an entirely new and unforeseen world, which only God has the wit and the wherewithal to bring about.

And so, what then is faith? The Epistle to the Hebrews defines it as "the assurance of things hoped for, the conviction of things not seen" (Heb 11:1). So powerful is the pull of this faith, Pope Benedict has told us, that it quite literally "draws the future into the present," giving us, he says, "something of the reality we are waiting for," so that it need never again be a blind groping in the dark.[8]

Isn't this precisely the faith and the hope that, taking hold of Mary at a level deeper even than that of her sister, sends her running off to Christ, determined on making a total gift of self? It is the grace of the purest possible readiness to receive whatever Jesus is prepared to give. Accordingly, she entrusts everything to him, evincing such complete and childlike confidence that Jesus himself is profoundly moved. For in seeing

---

8. *Spe Salvi*, no. 7.

the face of her grief, that depthless human misery for which there is no remedy in this world, Jesus knows that it was for this reason that he came into the world to live and to die.

Once again, then, there is no way to the Father that may sidestep the Son. Nor may it circumvent the Cross. That is because Bethany is but a waystation along the route to Calvary, the place where Jesus will open the very heart of God for a world bleeding to death by its sin and sorrow.

O most compassionate Father, your Son, Jesus, opened the very heart of God to those who suffer. May our tears move you to look with tender mercy upon the sufferings that have for too long rent our own poor hearts.

CHAPTER 12

Where God Weeps

[Jesus] said, "Where have you laid him?" [The Jews who had come with Mary] said to him, "Lord, come and see." Jesus wept.

—Jn 11:34–35

When asked if it were necessary to fortify the mind before the approach of death, Dr. Johnson is reported to have replied with some asperity: "No, Sir, let it alone. It matters not how a man dies, but how he lives. The act of dying is not of importance, it lasts so short a time."[1] He has a point, certainly, but it is not one that the family of Lazarus would care to raise. Two sisters having just stood by helpless watching their brother die, the only question on their minds is—*why*?

---

1. James Boswell, *The Life of Samuel Johnson, LL.D* (New York: Henry Holt and Company, 1882), p. 195.

As the song says, "You're four days late and all hope is gone. Lord, we don't understand why you waited so long."[2]

Good point. And even if, in the very next stanza, closure is reached ("But his way is God's way, not yours or mine. And isn't it great when he's four days late, he's still on time!"), the question will not go away. What was Jesus thinking? Could he not have come sooner? And when he finally does show up, does he do anything? No, he does not. He merely weeps.

And while it may be tempting to ask how helpful are tears when what is really needed is action, the impulse needs to be resisted. Because these are the tears of God, which invite us to examine more deeply the source of his sorrow, to glimpse the grief of God's own heart laid bare before us. Yes, it is true, that from the moment Jesus arrives in Bethany, following an absence of four days that surely feels like forever, he wants to know only one thing: "Where have you laid him?" And when the Jews, who have come to commiserate with the family, tell him, there is this absolutely stunning scene in which God actually weeps.

2. Karen Peck and New River, "Four Days Late" (Daywind, 2000).

Why exactly is that so extraordinary? Because here the *Supreme Someone*, who stands in effortless and eternal transcendence to all that is human and created, all at once is reduced to tears. Why, it's positively unseemly. God is made to cry by the death of a mere mortal? How can that be? Haven't we all been given to understand that God is *impassible,* that because he is beyond change, no suffering may touch him? To witness the Lord of the universe, therefore, the very *Pantocrator* himself, actually shedding tears, why, it beggars belief.

But perhaps there is a way of getting a handle on the question that will nether undermine, nor even inconvenience, the fixed attributes of God. Try to imagine, says Rabbi Abraham Heschel, the distinguished scholar and theologian, two very disparate views of the world that confronted the patriarch Abraham.[3] And that in each of the two scenarios God—that is, *Yahweh*, the Father and Lord of Israel—is required to be fully present if the Jews, the People of the Promise, are to exist, indeed, to prevail. It cannot be permitted, in other words, for the one whom

---

3. Quoted in *A Passion for Truth* (New York: Farrar, Strauss and Giroux, 1973), p. 273.

God had appointed to look after his chosen people, to admit for a moment that the least velleity of indifference should mark the mind of Yahweh.

And so, pursuant to all this, Abraham is first shown a vision of "infinity, beauty, and wisdom," which moves him to ask if it be possible for such grandeur to exist without a God to whom we might turn and give thanks. It is only in an atheistic world, after all, that we are obliged to refuse to say thanks. Not even if your wife or best friend were to pass you enough mustard with which to festoon your hotdog, are you to give thanks. It is the worst moment in the life of the atheist, someone once said, when he is moved to give thanks and there is no one around to thank.

But now suppose, Heschel continues, that you find yourself in a very different world, one which is "engulfed in the flames of evil and deceit." The cry of the heart would then not be that of jubilation, but of anguish, of beseeching the heavens to answer the most excruciating question of all: Is it possible that there is no God "to take this misfortune to heart?" Not to be able to turn to a God willing to bear all that impacted sorrow and sin, a God so insouciant as to leave even his beloved Israel to the prey of her enemies, shorn of all hope and consolation? Life would be unendurable. Better to slit all our throats than to live in a world without God.

Either way, concludes Heschel, the existence of a good and gracious and merciful God—a God who is free to weep and is moved to do so—remains a necessary axiom on which all human life depends. This is precisely why, in this great work of his called *The Prophets*,[4] he will insist that the sorrows of Israel have become, quite literally, God's own grief. "No words have ever gone further in offering comfort when the sick world cries out," he says of Isaiah. For too long the voice of Yahweh kept silent. But now, Heschel reminds us, *like a woman in travail*, God will cry out. It is, he tells us, "the boldest figure" used by anyone to describe God's tender mercies, the sheer depthless solicitude and solidarity struck between God and the people he loves.

In his moving encyclical *On Christian Hope*, Benedict XVI makes the point that God, while he cannot suffer in himself, in the eternity of his being God, is nevertheless free to suffer with all that is not God, reminding us that, indeed, so precious are

---

4. (New York: Harper & Row, 1962), pp. 145 and 151.

we in his sight, so imperishably important are we to God, that he became man precisely in order to prove it. The incarnation of God is not a statement about God, it is a showing—a *monstration*—by God, a dramatization, no less, of how far God is prepared to go in his determination to share our pain. Not to rid us of it in some cheap magical way, but to enter fully into it, reaching right down into the very marrow of our brokenness and misery, and there to redeem and sanctify the whole of it. "Hence in all human suffering," Benedict reminds us, "we are joined by one who experiences and carries that suffering with us; hence *con-solatio* is present in all suffering, the consolation of God's compassionate love—and so the star of hope rises."[5]

How else are we to imagine Jesus Christ if not as the protagonist in a series of dramatic descents, each progressively deeper into the dust, unto the very limit of finite and broken being? Yes, he is going to the Father, but always he goes by way of us, unto the very seat of our wretchedness, whence to pry us loose from its hellish hold. "How little we understand the Passion of Christ," writes Fr. Gerald Vann,

---

5. Benedict XVI, *Spe Salvi*, no. 39.

unless we understand at least that! If holiness did mean possessing God we might well despair; but holiness means being possessed by God . . . the Word is long since descended into us: there is nothing there that can frighten him now.[6]

I so cherish that passage from the philosopher Wittgenstein, which I came across while reading Heather King. "The Christian religion," he says, is only for one who needs infinite help . . . who feels infinite anguish. The whole earth can suffer no greater torment than a *single* soul. The Christian faith—as I see it—is one's refuge in this ultimate torment." And why not? Here is this Jesus guy, as Ms. King tells it,

> who hung out with lepers, paralytics, the possessed: this is someone I can trust. We don't have to go up to him, he comes down to us. We want a doctor, a hospital, meds; he gives himself. We want to stop the suffering; he says, *I'll suffer with you.*[7]

There can be no greater sign of solidarity, of sheer divine kinship, of God's complete identification with

---

6. From *The Water and the Fire* (New York: Sheed and Ward, 1954), p. 40.

7. From her book *Redeemed: Stumbling Toward God, Sanity, and the Peace That Passes All Understanding* (New York: Penguin, 2008), p. 1.

the children of men, than the tears of Jesus, so copiously shed at the death of his friend. A God who will not weep for the children who are lost is no better than the god of Aristotle—or the clockmaker god of the Deists—an unmoved mover whom no one is moved to love.

✦ Father of mercy and love, we thank you for the tears of Jesus, which he freely shed on behalf of all who undergo pain and death.

CHAPTER 13

On the Wings of Hope

So the Jews said, "See how he loved him!" But some of them said, "Could not he who opened the eyes of the blind man have kept this man from dying?"

—Jn 11:36–37

In looking over the course of his life, which was both long and productive, author and convert Malcolm Muggeridge made a striking discovery. He had at last realized, he said,

> that the only thing that's taught one anything is suffering, not success, not happiness, not anything like that. The only thing that really teaches one what life's about— the joy of understanding, the joy of coming in contact with what it really signifies—is suffering, is affliction.[1]

---

1. From an episode of *Firing Line* with William F. Buckley Jr. on "Faith and Religious Institutions," 1981. The whole exchange can be found in

If we are to understand our lives, therefore—and it is surely at the heart of the Christian message that we do so—it is because we've accustomed ourselves to seeing everything in dramatic terms, in which two alternating currents of joy and woe course through everything. "Life is not tragedy," says Luigi Giussani. "Tragedy is what makes everything amount to nothing. Life is a drama. It is dramatic because it is the relationship between our I and the You of God." On this point everything impinges. "It is this Presence, this You that makes circumstances change, because without this You everything would be nothing, everything would be a step toward an ever darker tragedy."[2]

Christ wants to be present and alive in everything. Yes, even amid the derelictions that so often pockmark the journey. Which is Muggeridge's larger point, of course: that if we really wish to acquire wisdom, then

---

Vintage Muggeridge: Religion and Society, edited by Geoffrey Barlow (Grand Rapids: Eerdmans, 1985). The specific discussion can be found in "How Does One Find Faith?" pp. 113–115. These exchanges are also referenced on the following page of this book.

2. Taken from "Notes of a Meditation on Recognizing Christ," in the booklet *From Faith, the Method: Exercises of the Fraternity of Communion and Liberation* (Rimini, Italy: Communion and Liberation, 2009), p. 5. The words are those of Julian Carron, who succeeded Msgr. Giussani as president of the Fraternity.

it will come through agony. In illustration of this he cites the character of Lear, and the awful tale of his own undoing, which is the theme of travail running through the entire play. "Let me tell you what will be a simple parable which I often thought of," he begins:

> Some very humane, rather simple-minded old lady sees the play *King Lear* performed, and she is outraged that a poor old man should be so humiliated, so made to suffer; and in the eternal shade she meets Shakespeare, and she says to him, "What a monstrous thing to make that poor old man go through all that." And Shakespeare says, "Yes, I quite agree. It was very painful, and I could have arranged for him to take a sedative at the end of Act I, but then, ma'am, there would have been no play."

The old king has simply got to submit to the suffering if he is to see the point of the play, whose meaning cannot be detached from the misery it documents. The overall design is in the details, every last one of which poor Lear must be made to endure. Thus, at play's end, when Lear delivers his final heartbreaking speech about he and Cordelia going off to prison together, and there "take upon's the mystery of things / As if we were God's spies," it is not an unearned wisdom, but acquired and deepened by an agony of soul which is the action of the play itself.

Which brings us back to Lazarus and the tears his passing prompts Jesus to shed. The inference, in seeing Jesus weep before the tomb of his dead friend, is that he obviously loved him. Those present certainly thought so. But some are clearly puzzled by the fact. Why hadn't he gone to the grave sooner, they want to know, thus preventing the poor fellow from having to die in the first place? Hadn't he performed plenty of miracles already? Why not this one? It's not as if the supply were limited. If one is God, after all, then there's nothing standing in the way.

Assume, then, that the tears are genuine, owing to the obvious sincerity of Christ's love for his friend. Owing also to the fact that Jesus is God, who is free to weep wherever there is pain and loss. The two, in fact, go together. "Love anything," C. S. Lewis tells us, "and your heart will certainly be wrung and possibly be broken. If you want to make sure of keeping it intact, you must give your heart to no one, not even to an animal."[3]

---

3. Cited by Josef Pieper in his section "On Love," from his book *Faith, Hope, Love* (San Francisco: Ignatius, 1997), p. 229.

The Lord of the universe is a lover, therefore, whose human heart, while joined hypostatically to the eternal Word, lies broken upon the wheel of a cruel and unjust world. And it is given to all. Faith has made that fact abundantly plain. Romano Guardini, in reflecting upon so many impossible things turning out well when seen from the perspective of faith, puts it this way: "How can the eternal God have created time and the finite? How could he have loved this perishable human creature planted on this atom of dust which is the earth? How is it possible for God to have become man?" For such things, he concludes, "faith has a ready answer full of sanctity: 'Love does such things.'"[4]

Meanwhile, the crowd is quite mistaken on the matter of the miracle they imagine Jesus might so easily have performed. "They are like pupils," writes Adrienne von Speyr, speaking of the spectators expecting Jesus to prop up poor Lazarus, "who have understood only one principle of geometry and now try to apply it everywhere."[5]

---

4. Cited in *The Magnificat Year of Faith Companion* (Oct. 11, 2012 to Nov. 24, 2013), from the Meditation for August 15, 2013, p. 328.

5. *John, Volume 2: The Discourses on Controversy*, trans. Brian McNeil, CRV (San Francisco: Ignatius, 1993), p. 367.

So, they would argue, having done one, why not many? They take no account of the mysterious dispositions of the Lord, which are simply not subject to human calculation. Not realizing that, as Gregory of Nyssa warns, "If all things were within our grasp, the Higher Power would not be beyond us."[6] They are like Dante, his mind fixated upon the appearance of God in the final lines of the *Paradiso*, yet too witless to speak a word. "My language now," he tells us, "will be more inadequate, / Even for what I remember, than would that / Of a child still bathing his tongue at the breast."[7]

An astonishing admission, to be sure, especially as so earthy an image is used in making it. But there he is, speechless before the two greatest possible mysteries, that of the Trinity and the Incarnation, knowing himself to be entirely unequal to the vision of either. Not only a God both one and three, which is confounding enough. But that on the very inside of so staggering a reality, he is given a sudden and piercing glimpse of the human being Jesus, "*painted*," as Dante stupefyingly

---

6. Hans Urs von Balthasar, *Presence and Thought: An Essay on the Religious Philosophy of Gregory of Nyssa* (San Francisco: Ignatius Press, 1995), 1.

7. From Canto 33 of the *Paradiso*.

tells us, "*with our effigy.*" This is the truly riveting event, which leaves him as helpless as the "geometer who sets himself / To square the circle, and is unable to think / Of the formula he needs to solve the problem." Not, he concedes, "a flight for my wings": "Except that my mind was struck by a flash / In which what it desired came to it."[8]

Thus seized in both mind and will by so dazzling a discovery, "high imagination" fails him entirely; nevertheless, his whole being will be "turned like a wheel, all at one speed, / By the love that moves the sun and the other stars."[9]

So too are the events before us. Overmastered by a God whose timetable it was never our business to know, we too must move in darkness, even as we long for flight into that final and still more dazzling darkness of which the dying and rising of Lazarus provides so tantalizing an intimation. After all, Jesus has promised to carry us there, and he longs to do so. But only to the degree we are willing to spread those wings of hope on which all celestial flight depends.

---

8. Dante, *Paradiso*, Canto 33.

9. Dante, *Paradiso*, Canto 33.

✦ Almighty Father, in allowing your servant Lazarus to die, you revealed the face of a compassionate Son with whom we had not reckoned. Teach us to be patient in accepting your will, especially when we do not understand your way.

CHAPTER 14

Dread of Death

Then Jesus, deeply moved again, came to the tomb; it was a cave, and a stone lay upon it. Jesus said, "Take away the stone." Martha, the sister of the dead man, said to him, "Lord, by this time there will be an odor, for he has been dead four days."

—Jn 11:38–39

What is it about the dead that makes us so fearful of them? Why should they, of all people, be a source of deep, unavailing dread? Not just physical fear or disgust, mind you, which is, after all, perfectly rational as it remains tethered to something real—like a scorpion, say, sheltering in your shoe. But dread is not at all like that, the fear and loathing it awakens having no object *out there* on which to fix the attention. And, yet, in all seriousness, there is nothing this side of a bunny rabbit or a titmouse less threatening than a corpse.

Besides, if Wittgenstein is to be believed,[1] death is not even an event of life. "Death is not lived through," he informs us. When it comes, it inflicts dread only if it sticks around, which of course it never does. And while we're at it, let us not forget the fact that being dead is no less ordinary or strange than being alive. It's a perfectly banal business, in fact, and when it happens why should anyone be surprised? For most of us, in fact, it will prove to be quite boringly predictable. Why, then, the fuss? Get a life!

And yet, all the same, death remains the least tolerable or welcome of all the various mishaps and calamities that manage to upend our lives. Not only is it incomprehensible, especially when *you* have been targeted, but insupportable as well. To the poor battered body, certainly, which may explain why it never survives the experience. "We die too quickly," reports Joseph Epstein, "or too slowly, drearily, painfully, sloppily, undignifiedly, horrendously, but—and here is the genuinely bad news—inevitably."[2] Small wonder, then, that the world's leading *thanatologist*, Dr. Elisabeth

---

1. See his *Tractatus Logico-Philosophicus* (*Treatise on Logic and Philosophy*) (England: Kegan Paul, 1922), prop. 6.4311, p. 87.

2. *Narcissus Leaves the Pool* (New York: First Mariner, 2007), p. 18.

Kübler-Ross, describes death as "a dreaded and unspeakable issue to be avoided by every means possible in our modern society."[3]

But, of course, it cannot be avoided, much less denied. Which is why those who dismiss the plain evidence of their senses on the grounds that only ideas are real—Bishop George Berkeley being the most famous example—remain exceedingly silly in their fanatical fixation upon ideas alone. Old Berkeley, by the way, was the fellow whom Boswell brought up in conversation with Dr. Johnson, whose doctrine he instinctively knew to be false but hadn't the wit to refute it. But Johnson did. "I never shall forget the alacrity with which Johnson answered, striking his foot with mighty force against a large stone, till he rebounded from it—'I refute it *thus*.'"[4]

Death is a fact and no sensible person will deny either that its ravages are real or terminal. And, yet, for most of us, we'd sooner not have to check out just this moment. Nor would we wish it to happen to those we love, which is to sound a theme far more telling. If

---

3. *Death: The Final Stage of Growth* (New York: Touchstone, 1986), p. 5.

4. Boswell, *Life of Samuel Johnson*, p. 142.

the best possible compliment we can pay to another human being is to say, "How good it is that you exist," what would be the worst? That it would be even better were you *not* to exist? But no lover would ever speak that way about his beloved. Indeed, he would most passionately declare the opposite: "How sad—how dreadfully, unspeakably sad—that you, of all people, should cease to be!"

This is why we are not resigned to die, why we mourn the death of others. We simply do not wish to go gently, as the poet Dylan Thomas famously put it, "into that good night."[5] Death is a problem for us, an outrage even, against the heart of what it means to be human, which is this yearning, this irrepressible desire, to live always and in communion with those we love. And, yes, without pain. Who wouldn't prefer a brightly colored door thrown open upon great sun-swept vistas of joy, to the wrenching prospect of being pitched overboard into the bottomless sea of death? Where there is only one direction, that of descent. Is there anyone who does not want to escape *the big sleep*? ("What did

---

5. Dylan Thomas, "Do Not Go Gentle into That Good Night," *The Poems of Dylan Thomas* (New York: New Directions, 1952).

it matter," asked Raymond Chandler, "where you lay once you were dead? [. . .] You just slept the big sleep, not caring about the nastiness of how you died or where you fell.")[6] But we do care. No one wants to fall haplessly into a black hole, where neither light nor love awaits the soul. Old Homer was not wrong when he wrote of Hades, fearful god of the underworld: "Men hate him most of all the gods."[7]

It was precisely into such a place that Jesus himself went in search of his dead friend. In looking over St. John's account, one notes the fetid air amid the stench of decaying flesh. We see Jesus as he trembles before the tomb, recoiling in his human nature from the sheer dread-inducing finality and terror of death, which makes cowards of us all.

The real horror of death, however, is not the rotting flesh; it is instead the soul's corruption, of which the physical signs of revulsion stand as an outward symbol. This is why, I expect, Jesus insists on our seeing the evidence of four dreadful days of decomposing flesh with our own eyes. But what Christ is really determined on

---

6. Chandler, *The Big Sleep*, chap. 32, 1939.

7. Homer, *The Iliad*, trans. W. H. D. Rouse (New York: Thomas Nelson and Sons, Ltd., 1938), book 9.

is stripping the soul itself, of laying it bare before us, of unmasking its disguise of flesh, beneath which the essence of sin, of saying no to God, to being, will no longer find refuge anywhere.

And so the Lord of light and life steps across the gate and into the grave of death, showing himself to be superior to the forces of darkness and sin. In a word, he goes *looking* for Lazarus, intent on bringing him back; not just to a state of renewed bodily being, but to that radiant and risen condition in which flesh and spirit are joined in a redeemed actuality, purchased, we must not forget, at the cost of his own life, his own death.

Here is the decisive sign: Christ impressing upon his dead friend the image and foreshadowing of all that he intends to accomplish in himself. Christ has come to raise us all from the ground, the dark abyss, into which, without exception, we have all fallen. That way, you see, each of our own deaths is given scope and space within the infinite reach of his own.

"So death will come to fetch you?" asks St. Thérèse of the Holy Face. "No, not death, but God himself."[8]

---

8. See her "Counsels and Memories," cited in *Death: A Book of Preparation and Consolation*, edited and compiled by Barry Ulanov (New York: Sheed & Ward, 1959), p. 22.

And so we need not fear if body and soul be separated for a time, never mind the sudden shock of dislocation for, in the perspective of eternity, it is fleeting indeed. A paltry price to pay, you might say, exacted ever so briefly, for what will unite us forever with God and with all those whom we are to love in and through God. Death holds no terror, in other words, for those who cling to Christ. For the heavenly Father, who is both his Father and ours, is a God on whom death has no lasting hold. It was the Father, after all, who sent his Son into the tomb where death holds sway, in order to deliver us from its myriad fears and terrors. We praise him thus for the unconquerable hope he has given us to put even the dread of death to flight.

➻ Heavenly Father, for whom only life is real and on whom death has no claim, you sent your Son and our Brother into the tomb where death reigns, in order to break his kingdom in two. We praise you for the hope you have given us to vanquish the darkness.

CHAPTER 15

Telling Lazarus to Get Up

Jesus said to [Martha], "Did I not tell you that if you would believe you would see the glory of God?" So they took away the stone. And Jesus lifted up his eyes and said, I thank thee that thou hast heard me. I knew that thou hearest me always, but I have said this on account of the people standing by, that they may believe that thou didst send me." When he had said this, he cried with a loud voice, "Lazarus, come out."

—Jn 11:40–43

The scene is dramatically set against the backdrop of a tomb where a man lies dead. He has been in the ground for four days, during which time nothing has happened at all, save the growing sound of lament voiced by family and friends haplessly awaiting the arrival of one on whom they had placed all their hopes.

But he does not come. Had they mistakenly hitched their wagon to the wrong star?

And when, finally, he does show up, what does he do? He engages the grieving sister in conversation. Telling her things so strange and astonishing that never in the history of the world has a human being ever spoken like that.

So, what exactly does Jesus tell Martha? How can mere words be said to assuage her sorrow? Indeed, a bitterness and misery that left to marinate after four days has got to be on the verge of open revolt. Will he not at least apologize for the delay in coming? No, he does not. Instead, he tells her that if only she were to believe, the glory of the Lord would be hers to see. It is an absolutely horizon-shattering statement, no greater than which could possibly be made. How does she react? Will she accept it? Does she in fact believe? The implication, of course, is that if she were to do so, the result would be nothing less than eternal beatitude, which is to say, the condition of actually seeing the glory—the very *kabod*, or *doxa*—of the Lord. Meanwhile, those who do not believe will, alas, never see.

Only then is the stone removed, allowing Jesus to cry out, "*Lazarus, come out!*"

In the midst of all this, an extraordinary exchange takes place between Jesus and his heavenly Father, hinting at layer upon layer of divine mystery. It is an even more amazing conversation than the one just concluded with the human being Martha. And it is one which all who have come to the tomb are privy to hear. That is because the one who speaks is the Eternal Word himself, the *Logos* of God, who is standing simultaneously before the crowd of mourners and this Absolute Other whom he addresses as Father, *Abba*.

Why would he be speaking to him? Because, quite simply—and from all eternity—he is his meat and drink, indeed, "the refulgence of his glory, the very imprint of his being," to recall the stirring passage from the beginning of the Letter to the Hebrews, "who sustains all things by his mighty word" (Heb 1:3, NABRE). Also because he, the Father, has sent him into the world in order that it might be persuaded to believe, to accept, as Martha herself does, the testimony of the Son on whom every assurance of beatitude is given to those who believe.

"The meaning of this Word," writes Hans Urs von Balthasar,

is inexhaustible and utterly profound . . . it can be ultimately interpreted only by means of itself. It contains latent within itself the fullness of the eternal life, the mysteries of heaven, the ocean of Trinitarian truth and love.[1]

From the very first moment God stoops to speak to us his Word, whose reach and resonance well up from the bottomless depths of the Godhead, there could never be another Word that God needed to speak, to give expression and voice to his mind or will. That he chose to speak this Word in time, amid the circumstances of a particular people ("How odd of God to choose the Jew!"), does not imply in any way an attenuation of that Word, as if time and the theater of human action in which its amplification is felt, had the power either to mute or to mitigate the immediacy of its impact and sound.

For as John's Gospel makes instantly clear, and profoundly arresting, right from the start, "In the beginning was the Word." John has thus set himself to scale the heights of a Christology no loftier than which can

---

1. Taken from *Love Alone: The Way of Revelation* (London: Sheed & Ward, 1968), pp. 41 and 42.

be imagined. And in this extraordinary exchange, this *dia-logos* between Jesus and the Father, the innermost secret of their unity stands revealed. "In this dynamic circle of Trinitarian love," Pope Benedict XVI declared while still a Cardinal, "there is the highest degree of unity and constancy."[2] It will be the animating source, no less, that sustains the whole universe; concerning which the crowd surrounding the tomb is privileged to overhear, eavesdropping, as it were, on a conversation whose depths it will never fathom. Nor anyone else, for that matter. Only the Word knows what is in the mind of God, even as in sounding its depths it has no other mind in mind.

Are we not all eavesdroppers, having looked through the lattice work between this world and the next, vouchsafed bits and pieces of a conversation we cannot altogether follow? It is one which is without beginning or end, evincing, from all eternity, a relation of knowledge and love so absolute and profound as to, quite literally, breathe forth the Holy Spirit. In the light of this event alone, not even the raising of a dead man back to life can compete.

---

2. Joseph Ratzinger, *Seeking God's Face*, trans. David Smith and Robert Cunningham (Chicago: Franciscan Herald, 1982), p. 37.

No single event in time, never mind how stupendous, can match the majesty of this moment. Here is God himself giving evidence of himself, thereby enabling us to witness the Incarnate Son giving thanks to the Father, in the very Spirit whom together they *spirate*. An eternal procession, no less, and it is from within this unheard-of crucible of unending life and love that all other mysteries derive. Mysteries of both creation and redemption. We've been shown here the merest hint or intimation of the central *theo-drama*, whose depths defy any man to plumb, reaching as they do into the Tri-Une heart of God. Here, then, is the point of origin, the eternal source on which the kenosis of Christ, the complete self-emptying of the Son, will necessarily depend. Here is the precise ground on which the great Pauline hymn of Philippians 2:8 will take its stand, revealing how God, "being found in human form humbled himself and became obedient unto death, even death on a cross." This profound drama, played out on the stage of human history, draws all its sustenance from an eternal drama performed by the Son of God for the love and delight of the Father. An eternal self-emptying, no less, for the sake of One who remains the perpetual font of his being.

No mortal is equal to an event of this magnitude: of seeing *who* Christ is, the relation he has from all eternity with the Father, and the love coursing through both in order to breathe forth the Spirit. All of it pursuant to a mission to the world of men, one of whom is at this moment in the ground, his spirit thirsting for resurrection. An amazing miracle is about to take place, replete with the most far-reaching implications for the children of men, their brief lives circumscribed by death. And only one person in the crowd has a clue as to what is about to happen.

If faith, as St. Paul reminds us, comes from what is heard, then the faith stirred into life by this miracle will surely testify to all that has been heard before, indeed, to the most foundational mystery of all, that of sheer, unending, reciprocal exchange within the Godhead, and without which nothing further is possible. Jesus is about to instruct Lazarus to get up and leave the tomb, and because, from all eternity, Jesus knows the Father is listening and that he knows and loves him, Lazarus will certainly do so.

And, to be sure, in telling Lazarus to get up, Jesus is also advising us, addressing each of us by name, to get up and leave as well. God longs for us all to climb out of the tomb, to emerge from whatever darkness enshrouds our lives. Lazarus, whose name means *God is my help*, is the prototype, if you will, who prefigures in his own body the mystery meant for all of us, the apt symbol of all that God has set himself to accomplish for those whom he loves.

➤ O Father of our Lord Jesus Christ, you speak the Word always, and you allow his voice to resound everywhere. Let us hear this Word that brings life and hope to the world.

CHAPTER 16

What the Dead Now Know

The dead man came out, his hands and feet bound with bandages, and his face wrapped with a cloth. Jesus said to them, "Unbind him, and let him go." Many of the Jews therefore, who had come with Mary and had seen what he did, believed in him; but some of them went to the Pharisees and told them what Jesus had done.

—Jn 11:44–46

When, late in his life, the novelist Graham Greene was asked if he wasn't disappointed at failing to win the Nobel Prize, he said that, well, actually, he was waiting for a much bigger prize. And what, he was then asked, might that be? "Death," he replied.[1]

---

1. Reported in the following article: Dinesh D'Souza, "Beyond Marx and Jesus: Is Death the Only Prize That Now Awaits Graham Greene?," *Crisis Magazine*, May 1, 1988, *https://www.crisismagazine.com/1988/beyond-marx-and-jesus-is-death-the-only-prize-that-now-awaits-graham-greene*.

Unless one knew something of the despair that dogged much of his life, one would think an even bigger surprise than death would be to survive it. In a word, to transcend death, and thus to be ushered into the kingdom of Heaven where, for all eternity, one is embraced by the arms of almighty God.

When Alfred Delp, the German Jesuit priest martyred by the Nazis in the final days of the Second World War, was about to be hanged, he reportedly turned to the prison chaplain who had accompanied him to the scaffold and, speaking confidingly to him, made the following prediction: "In half an hour, I'll know more than you do."[2]

When my father died a few years back and, following the Mass of Christian Burial, I was asked to say a few words about him, I quoted that text, which I found, and still do, deeply moving. What did Fr. Delp know? And how could he have been so confident in knowing it? I pray that my father now knows it as well. And that all of us might someday know it, too.

---

2. As recorded in the biography of Alfred Delp: Mary Frances Coady, *With Bound Hands: A Jesuit in Nazi Germany: the Life and Selected Prison Letters of Alfred Delp* (Chicago: Loyola Press, 2003), p. 207.

And what about Lazarus? Did he, on his return, have anything new to say, some startling piece of intelligence that only the dead can know? What is the world C. S. Lewis once described as "beyond the wardrobe" really like? In a moving poem called "A View of Lazarus," Elizabeth Jennings puts it this way: "A look of loss," she writes,

Shows on his features but he does not speak.
Some begin to question him about
What dying felt like
[. . .]
But he seems dumb and we don't want to make
His rising difficult although we long
To look back at the glimmering kingdom he
Has left, if Paradise is there
But is not for the snatching.[3]

So why hasn't Lazarus, who clearly did come back, why does he not tell us anything? "What difference," asks Fr. Gerald Vann in his book *The Divine Pity*, "did

---

3. Elizabeth Jennings, "A View of Lazarus," *New Collected Poems* (Manchester: Carcanet, 1995), p. 311.

his journey into eternity make to him?" Couldn't he have at least sent a postcard? We are left, in fact, with only a single scrap of information, namely a supper at which both he and the Lord are present, and not a word does Lazarus speak. Not even a peep. What sort of dream state was the poor fellow in? "You imagine," suggests Fr. Vann, "the practical, motherly Martha having to tell him repeatedly: 'Lazarus, do get on with your food.'"[4]

"It was the amazing white," begins another poem by Elizabeth Jennings, this one simply titled "Lazarus," in which we are repeatedly reminded that he will not speak, that

> it was the way he simply
> Refused to answer our questions, it was the cold
>   pale glance
> Of death upon him, the smell of death that truly
> Declared his rising to us.
> [. . .]
> This man was dead, I say it again and again.

4. *The Divine Pity: A Study in the Social Implications of the Beatitudes* (Glasgow: Collins, 1945), p. 1.

All of our sweating bodies moved towards him.
And our minds moved too, hungry for finished faith.
He would not enter our world at once with words
That we might be tempted to twist or argue with:
Cold like a white root pressed in the bowels of earth
He looked, but also vulnerable—like birth.[5]

Leaving Lazarus' silence to one side, which may
well have lasted the balance of his life, in the final verses
of chapter eleven we are shown a most riveting scene,
which brings dramatically to a close the longest-running
narrative of the New Testament (with the exception,
that is, of the Lord's passion). Answering the summons
of the Lord, Lazarus appears wrapped in his winding
sheet of death. Seeing him thus tightly bound, Jesus
turns to the attendants of the grave. "Untie him," he
commands. And all at once the dead man is returned
to life. Brought suddenly forth from the tomb of darkness, Lazarus is welcomed into the light of day, before
whom stands the source of all light. Christ, the true
Lumen Gentium, who, in all his blazing incandescence,
brings life out of death, hope springing forth from an

---

5. Jennings, "Lazarus," *New Collected Poems*, p. 48.

abyss of despair. Who can imagine such prodigies? It is the most astounding life-transforming moment anyone could imagine, one which, unless one were entirely catatonic, changes everything.

One thinks of Chesterton's quip, that the reason angels can fly is because they take themselves lightly. How lightly, one wonders, will Lazarus be taking himself after all this? It puts one in mind of the famous figure in bronze sculpted by Jacob Epstein, adorning the antechapel of New College, Oxford, in which the freshly resuscitated corpse is freed from all that had bound him. Not just the weight of death, but also sin and sorrow, the whole bloody burden of having to live in a fallen and wretched world, all at once lifted and thrown effortlessly away. As if an old tattered shirt were suddenly made new, wrinkle-free too.

How wonderfully it reminds us that such oppressions as sin and death need not be the last word. Because Christ, in freely assuming our death, taking ownership of our sin, utterly vanquished the destructive power unleashed by each of these ancient enemies. Christ paid a debt he did not owe, because we had a debt we could not pay. Lazarus is his first down payment on a victory intended for us all.

Leaving but one question, which has long tormented many. How, in all seriousness, could anyone refuse an offer so obviously, so extravagantly, over-the-top? Why, when God in his heaven beckons the soul made in his image, would anyone turn away, taking himself to a place of unending horror and shame? A state of being lost, of utter forlornness, no human being was ever created to have to endure? To say no to God at the last seems not merely stupid, but positively suicidal.

On the other hand, many do believe, and despite the depredations and seductions of the world and the flesh and the devil, persist in their hunger and thirst for God, revealing the sheer depth of their desire for life, for a destiny which death cannot finally touch. "In all their celebrations," writes Joseph Ratzinger,

> men have always searched for that life which is greater than death. Man's appetite for joy, the ultimate quest for which he wanders restlessly from place to place, only makes sense if it can face the question of death.[6]

---

6. *The Feast of Faith: Approaches to a Theology of the Liturgy* (San Francisco: Ignatius, 1986), pp. 150–151.

This is why we should be glad, and most grateful, too, for Christ's conquest of death, his overcoming of the power of sin that leads ineluctably to it. Because it has freed us all. Save only those whose number—please God, may it be few—remain perversely determined on a condition of darkness which, for all that Christ came to free us from it, they would sooner have than him. For what other reason are the doors leading into Hell locked on the inside?

→ O God and Father of all the living, your Son brought Lazarus back to life. Make us heirs of this same life so that in Jesus, in the life of the Spirit he breathed into the world, death will have no dominion.

EPILOGUE

Shall I tell you what makes for ideal entertainment in today's culture? The undeniable formula for television success? The answer is an absolute, unmitigated disaster, followed by a perfectly happy ending. Apply that standard to Lazarus and you've got a surefire hit.

How does the story end? Let us, as they say, count the ways. To begin with, you've got this miracle man, Jesus, who shows up to awaken this poor guy from the sleep of death. An event so startlingly unexpected that no audience would dream of leaving the theater. Everyone is there hanging on every word. And in his best James Earl Jones voice, he cries out the dead man's name. "*Lazarus*," he shouts, "*come out!*"

And, of course, he dutifully does. Only to be greeted with wild and joyous acclaim by all who know and love him. There he remains until, following the usual long and happy life, God calls him home for good. Nothing left to be done but go and pick up the Emmy.

In the real story, of course, nothing more is said on the matter at all. Meanwhile, let's not forget that there is another Lazarus in the New Testament, about whom a very different story is told. Although, between the two, there is one striking parallel, which is instructive enough because they each turn on the mystery of death. Oh, yes, and life—the unforeseen renewal of which comes out of death.

In the Gospel of St. Luke (16:19–31), we meet this wretched man named Lazarus, whom the rich man named Dives disdains to feed, leaving him to the ministrations of dogs, who lick his sores while Dives feasts on the finest wines and sweetbreads. In due course, they each die, the one bound for Heaven while the other falls into Hell. Amid the torments of the latter Dives cries out to Father Abraham, in whose bosom Lazarus sleeps, begging to please send Lazarus, "to dip the tip of his finger in water and cool my tongue, for I am suffering torment in these flames."

But Abraham refuses, reminding Dives of all the good things he had in life, while poor Lazarus languished in misery due to his indifference. Besides which, he adds, there is this fixed, unalterable abyss separating the two, which, for all eternity, prevents either one from crossing to the other side. Then, asks Dives, could Abraham not at least send him to his five other brothers, as wicked as he, to warn them of the fires awaiting them as well? Abraham thereupon issues his final refusal: "If they do not hear Moses and the prophets, neither will they be convinced if some one should rise from the dead" (Lk 16:31).

Could this, I wonder, have been the Lazarus whom the poet Eliot had in mind in writing "The Love Song of J. Alfred Prufrock"?[1] There we read the following: "I am Lazarus, come from the dead, / Come back to tell you all, I shall tell you all."

But, of course, Lazarus tells us nothing. Not certainly to those desiccated figures—"the women," for instance, who "come and go / Talking of Michelangelo"—who move through life with aimless and frivolous intent. To such as these, alas, poor Prufrock cannot bring himself to speak. And besides, he asks himself,

> would it have been worth it, after all,
>
> After the cups, the marmalade, the tea.
>
> Among the porcelain, among some talk of you and me,
>
> Would it have been worth while,

---

1. T. S. Eliot, "The Love Song of J. Alfred Prufrock," *Prufrock and Other Observations* (London: The Egoist, 1917), 9–16.

To have bitten off the matter with a smile,

To have squeezed the universe into a ball

To roll it toward some overwhelming question,

To say, "I am Lazarus, come from the dead,

Come back to tell you all, I shall tell you all."

No, it would not have been worthwhile. Not among these bored drawing-room creatures, who wander about already half-dead. As for Prufrock himself, the poor fellow hasn't enough moral starch in his shirt to accost anyone about anything. "Should I," he asks in his usual anemic way, "after tea and cakes and ices, / Have the strength to force the moment to its crisis?" No, he has not. A man whose life is "measured out . . . with coffee spoons," will not be taking on the universe anytime soon. Nor one whose affectations, while amusing, mask a deep and abiding aversion to asking first questions.

Shall I part my hair behind? Do I dare to eat
   a peach?

I shall wear white flannel trousers, and walk upon
   the beach.

In other words, it does not finally matter which Lazarus Eliot had in mind when casting about for the character. Poor Prufrock, his paltry little drama will never be the stuff of heroism.

So, what is this "overwhelming question" that he will not ask? To be sure, it is a question that other Lazarus, the one whose story John spends an entire chapter embroidering upon, does not ask, either, having returned mute from his sojourn among the shades. But we may ask it, indeed, we are constrained to do so. That is because, unlike the animals who never think, we are always thinking. "When an animal has nothing to do," suggests the Canadian Jesuit Bernard Lonergan, "it goes to sleep. When a man has nothing to do, he may ask questions."[2] Questions, moreover, which cast a piercing light upon the universe in which we live. Why else would we throw open the window on the world, if not because we are driven by wonder to know something of what's out there, its point of origin and nature and finality?

Who has not asked, for example, *Why is there being rather than nothingness?*[3] "The question of being is the darkest question in all philosophy," William James

2. Bernard Lonergan, *Insight: A Study of Human Understanding* (New York: Philosophical Library, 1958), p. 10.

3. See John Holt's book *Why Does the World Exist?: An Existential Detective Story* (New York: W. W. Norton & Company, 2012).

assures us.[4] Is it not, after all, every bit as plausible that nothing need be? Jean-Paul Sartre certainly thought so, telling us at great and learned length how "nothingness haunts being."[5] The nothingness, in other words, that could so easily have been, as opposed to the being that simply *is*.

It is because we think, therefore, that we ask questions. Indeed, says Pascal, "Man is a thinking reed."[6] Which is why, in the *Pensées*, his unfinished masterpiece in defense of the Christian religion, he tells us that it will never do to look for one's dignity in space. "It will do me no good to own land," he says. After all, such things as space—and time, too—consume us all. Ah, but in my thoughts, in the ordering of my mind, I may master the universe. "Through space the universe grasps me and swallows me up like a speck; through thought I grasp it."[7]

The exercise of the mind, therefore, puts us precisely in the line of reason's fire. Then we are face to face with

4. William James, *Some Problems of Philosophy* (New York: Longmans, Green, and Co., 1911), p. 46.

5. Jean-Paul Sartre, *Being and Nothingness*, trans. Hazel E. Barnes (New York: Citadel Press, 1953) pt. 1, chap. 1.

6. *Pensées*, no. 347.

7. No. 200.

the religious sense, which is the title of a splendid little book by Luigi Giussani, in which the reader is exhorted over and over to ask the most basic question of all, *What is the meaning of everything*? The religious sense, he explains, "appears as the first and most authentic application of the term *reason* because it never ceases responding relentlessly to reason's most basic need, for meaning."[8]

And what is another word for meaning but truth, which is the most apt synonym for Word, *Logos*, God. Almost without knowing it, one has entered the realm of prayer, of talking to God. In tripping over the wire of word, we encounter *Word*, are thrown into the space where God is present. He who alone exists, indeed, whose very *is-ing* is the energy on which everything else exists. I AM WHO I AM. Thus speaks the God of Moses when the latter puts the question to him, "What is your name?" (See Ex 3:13–14). And so I come back, one final time, to Lazarus, the friend and brother whom Jesus has brought so stunningly back to life. An absolutely astonishing story. But two things about it seem to me especially relevant—in fact, so strikingly salient that they will not go away. The first is the fact

---

8. *The Religious* Sense, p. 99.

of Jesus weeping on hearing the news. He really does weep when told that his friend Lazarus has died. This is surely incredible. That God himself, the *Alpha* and the *Omega* of the universe—who, in the human being Jesus becomes one of us, entering fully into the flesh and blood of our brokenness—should actually weep for a dead man. That real tears should fall down his face, and that in the sadness, the awful *pathos* of human loss, God is so fully invested that he *feels* our pain by having first made it his own. "Although he is God," declares St. Zeno of Verona, a fourth-century bishop and martyr,

> he takes suffering onto himself like a weak human being. He does this to put an end to the law of death and to enable us to share in immortality. God's power is this: that he can be what he is not and yet still remain what he is. . . . He is God and he is human, because he stands in the middle, between the Father and us. The reality of his flesh is revealed in his weakness and the reality of his majesty is revealed in his miracles.[9]

---

9. See Brian Linerd, ed., *A Way to the Heart of Christmas* (Hyde Park, N.Y.: New City Press, 1991).

The cries of Martha and Mary, so deep and uncontrived, mingle with those of Jesus, which tell us that in all who suffer, Christ suffers too. Pope Francis, in his reflection on the Second Beatitude, "Blessed are those who mourn, for they shall be comforted," said something that has stayed with me. When the human heart bleeds for another, he said, it must be "a question of loving the other in such a way that we are bound to him or her until we share his or her pain . . . that others make a breach in our hearts."[10]

Is this not how God loves all of us? That Jesus, in the tears shed for his friend, shows us the extent of the breach we have made in God's own heart?

Then there is this last detail, which I can no more put out of my head than the sight of those tears streaming down the face of Jesus. It is the fact that in going to Lazarus, in his willingness to face the corpse, from which following those four days in the tomb any sentient being would recoil, Jesus fully enters into that cave where, on the inside, he faces the decay and the rot of a dead man. And simply tells him to get up and walk out. The hideousness of the scene does not affect

---

10. General Audience, (December 2, 2020). Vatican website: *www.vatican.va*.

him at all; he is not offended or put off by the stench. He simply chooses to walk into that cave of darkness and putrefaction, and there amid the obvious revulsion awakened by the sight of death, commands that Lazarus return to life. What an inspired metaphor for the many dark caves in which we dwell! To pry us loose from the sins that bind us, to cleanse us of the filth and stench of the sins we commit, Christ reaches right down, entering into even the deepest of caves in order to call us out.

Is it possible, I wonder, that when it comes to death and dying, we become far too easily overwrought? Why can't we just put on the mind of Christ, who, in the face of our ancient enemy—"the ugly customer," Hazlitt called him[11]—evinced no fear whatsoever? Sheer unflappable confidence. Even the dread nothingness of death leaves him entirely undaunted. As if he were totally and serenely its master, putting to flight such fear and anxiety as all too often appear to undermine our own poor efforts, causing us to cower and cringe before his empty threats.

---

11. The English literary critic Henry Hazlitt, in his lecture "On Chaucer and Spenser" (1818).

Did I say empty? Yes, because when Christ came into the world, it was in order to conquer sin and death, to break their sham kingdom in two. How beautifully this is borne out by the example of Lazarus! "*Our friend Lazarus is asleep*," he tells his disciples, "*but I am going to awaken him*." In their obtuseness, they imagine that Jesus is speaking as though Lazarus had merely gone to bed, and so are baffled because it would hardly seem necessary then to go and wake him. But, no, Jesus tells them plainly, *Lazarus has died*. But he who holds the keys of death (see Rev 1:17–18), knows how to unlock that door, and thus set free its victims imprisoned therein.

Or, yet again, in the episode with the daughter of Jairus, reported in Matthew (9:24), Jesus informs the crowd, "*The girl is not dead but sleeping*." Here, again, the people appear incredulous, while others openly ridicule Jesus. But mightn't that be because their view of death is entirely defective? To our human eyes, sadly myopic as they are, death always appears undefeated; it is we who imagine death has come to vanquish us, our sins having been the wages we squander in advance. But not for Christ, who does things to death that make it die.

Why not, therefore, ask the question put by the poet Francis Quarles,

> Why should we not, as well desire death,
> As sleep? No difference, but a little breath;
> 'Tis all but rest; 'tis all but a releasing
> Our tired limbs; why then not alike pleasing?[12]

The poem ends by reminding us, once more, of that hidden and mysterious kinship between the two, which Christ by his coming among us has cemented forever:

> In sleep, we know not whether our closed eyes
> Shall ever wake; from death we're sure to rise:
> Aye, but 'tis long first; O is that our fears?
> Dare we trust God for nights? and not for years?

How sensible and wise Augustine was when he wrote: "To his sisters Lazarus was dead; to the Lord, he was only sleeping."

---

12. Francis Quarles, "On Death," in *Words of Comfort: for the Wayfarer, the Weary, the Sick, and the Aged*, ed. John Morris (Cambridge: Deighton, Bell, and Co., 1866), p. 459.

Or, Thérèse of Lisieux, who armed with so boundless a sense of hope that on its strength the Church has declared her a Doctor, to whom I shall give the last word. "So death will come to fetch you?" she asks.

No, not death, but God himself. Death is not the horrible spectre we see represented in pictures. The catechism teaches that death is the separation of the soul from the body; that is all. I am not afraid of a separation which will unite me forever with God.[13]

---

13. "Counsels and Memories," cited in *Death: A Book of Preparation and Consolation*, p. 22.